First responders are faced with dramatic and emotional calls throughout their careers which affect their mental health like no other in society. Often, we compartmentalize to try and cope with the effects. Gary provides deep personal insight into how devastating these calls affect your mind, body and spirit.

Any first responder reading his story will immediately recognize and reflect on their own personal demons in their career. Thankfully, Gary was able to overcome his own personal battles and provide reflection, self-awareness, and healing. *A Call for Service* will help you understand, and acquire perspective to realize healing can occur and you're not alone.

Michael Elliott
President - Edmonton Police Association
Director - Canadian Police Association

A Call for Service is an exceptional book giving us a rare view and subsequent insight into the lives of all of our frontline workers. While clearly based on the trials and struggles from a police perspective, I can absolutely relate to the stories and struggles in this book as a Firefighter Paramedic. For the everyday person, it shows the concept of what it is like to put your life on the line every day you go to work and its real perspective. The humanity and empathy shown for people in all kinds of states is incredible. This book reminded me that we all have our own struggles and our own journey. It also gives options to start your own journey in building resiliency and overcoming any personal demons you may have. A great read!

Matthew Wood
Firefighter/Paramedic
Mindset coach/speaker

A Call for Service written by Sergeant Gary Benoit is a testament to the front-line public servants who put their lives and their hearts in danger, every single day, to protect and serve their communities. Written with honesty and heart, we can feel the genuine emotions as well as the traumas that have affected Gary, his family, and his team within the force. Many people will never truly understand how these men and women struggle to find balance. Gary's integrity and focus on becoming the best version of himself, for his wife and son, for his parents, and for the people he serves, shines through in his life story. I was moved to hear his voice, his humor, and his strength of being reflected throughout the pages. The work he and his wife Colette are doing, in creating awareness for front-line workers will make a world of difference for everyone who struggles with mental health, with finding supports appropriate to their unique situations, and with the resiliency to carry on in a job that has so many challenges. Dear reader, if you ever find yourself in one of these places, please do not hesitate to reach out. There is a community of people who will hold you up. I promise you are not alone.

Reanna Erixon,
Senior Marketing Director, Success by Design Financial Counsellor, Mental Health Educator, Mother and Friend

This book is a must-read for anyone who has experienced trauma and is looking for a way out. *A Call for Service* will take you on a journey that will have you thinking about your own life and discovering a path to new healing.

Dr. Dave Braun
Co-founder of Oola
3X International Best-Selling Author
Social Media Influencer
Personal Growth Expert
World-renowned Work-Life Balance Expert

I want to thank Gary Benoit for being so open, honest and vulnerable. It must have taken tremendous courage to share his story and because of this many people will be able to relate to it and use his wisdom in their own healing journeys. I found that parts of the story were difficult to read as it brought up some emotions and similar memories for me but I also found it hard to put down. There were so many accounts of obstacles and difficult situations that he encountered but always remained resilient and determined to find the solutions or a positive outcome.

Gary's story creates a sense of hope and encouragement to keep moving forward and improve on life in the present and future. I appreciate the examples given, the honesty of his feelings at the moment and the hindsight that he acknowledged that could have led to different outcomes had he known better at the time. So many of us hold onto guilt, shame or loss of confidence but he has shown that there is a way to get past that and live a happy and grateful life. I look forward to using some of the tools he has provided in *A Call for Service* and want to thank Gary for having the strength to step forward and show us the way towards healing and post-traumatic growth.

I am grateful for Gary and his wisdom.

Trudy
Ex-Corrections Officer

A CALL FOR SERVICE

OVERCOMING ADVERSITY THROUGH RESILIENCE

GARY BENOIT

A Call for Service: Overcoming Adversity through Resilience

Benoit, Gary
ISBN 978-1-7782258-0-2 (Paperback)
ISBN 978-1-7782258-1-9 (eBook)
ISBN 978-1-7782258-2-6 (Paperback IS)

Edited by Christine Bode, Bodacious Copy.
Book Production by Dawn James, Publish and Promote.
Cover design by Publish and Promote.
Cover art by Vitaliy Paykov.
Interior layout and design by Perseus Design.

Printed and bound in Canada.

Note to the reader:
The events in this book are based on the author's memories from his perspective. The information is provided for educational and inspirational purposes only. The content is not intended as a substitute for professional advice, diagnosis, or treatment. Always seek the advice of your mental health professional or another qualified health provider with any questions you may have regarding your condition.

Dedication

I dedicate this book to my wife, Colette, and son, Aiden, for always being there for me. You are my catalyst for change and inspiration to keep growing and healing.

Acknowledgments

I want to add special thanks to Oola Guys, Dr. Dave and Dr. Troy; thank you for your guidance and friendship and for spreading Oola to the world. Thank you to Stacey Berger and EverExpanding Coaching for your wisdom and for asking me what I would love! Thank you to Vesna Bidniak for helping with smoothing out the rough draft of this book. Your initial edits and work were amazing.

Contents

Introduction

This book aims to provide all those who read it with the hope that things can be different in their lives if they decide to change. Specifically, the change that can happen is as wide-ranging as one can dream. You can change your financial status, relationships, and job satisfaction, build resilience and mental well-being, or it could be something as simple as increasing your happiness in life. I designed it for the reader and shared my stories to allow readers to connect with their stories to know they are not alone in their daily struggles with an occupational stress injury (OSI). Even if you do not have an OSI, this book can help anyone find more purpose and passion for the life they are living right now. The strategies in this book took me from feeling broken by my OSI— feeling I had lost direction in life, disconnected and angry at everything—to the person I am today, a happy, resilient, grounded, positive person full of purpose.

I am confident that if you put effort into these same strategies, you will see positive change in your life. *A Call for Service* does not replace seeking professional help if you require it, and I always encourage you to seek that help. Reading this book will assist your recovery journey through an OSI and allow the reader to reflect on their life and career. I want you to reflect with grace and self-forgiveness. Hopefully, it will enable you to start conversations with those closest to you. I want to change the focus from the stigma associated with mental health to a path of healing and normalcy. I would love every reader to be inspired by this book, start setting goals for themselves, and know they can live a life full of purpose, passion, and happiness. I know it sounds cliché, but it truly is about the journey, not the destination. The journey is not about perfection; it is about progress! We only have a finite amount of time on this rock, and we all deserve to live out our time in a way that brings us the most joy, invites in the most love and creates the most memories. I hope you enjoy this book and wish you the best in life ahead.

CHAPTER 1

On Patrol

On a cold December night in 2007, I was about to start my regular tour of four patrol shifts in the city of Edmonton. As I prepared to head to work, it was no different from any other day. I had minimal sleep the night before and was up in the morning with the family. I packed a lunch and had my police uniforms ready to put into the bag. I always fold the shirts and then roll them up to try and avoid wrinkles. I roll up my pants for the same reason. I take pride in the uniform and don't like it when it wrinkles. I have no idea if rolling up the clothes works, but I've done that from my first days on patrol, and I still do it now.

As I headed into the station that night, I felt groggy, but the closer I got to work, the more awake I became. The adrenaline started to flow, my heart rate increased, and my body tingled. It is funny, but no matter how tired I feel at home, the minute I start commuting to work, I begin to wake up, and my entire body comes alive.

When I arrived at work, I changed into my uniform, put on my duty belt, and headed to the parade table for our usual pre-shift briefing. I couldn't wait to head out and grab a coffee to get things going for the set. That day on parade, my sergeant spoke about the procedures required when there is an officer-involved shooting. He reviewed this to prepare us for what happened procedurally after that type of event. He brought this topic up to check new, recently introduced procedures because of the increased likelihood of experiencing that event (due to increased violence in the city). I had no idea how meaningful that conversation and information would be seven hours later into my shift.

That night my shift started as usual. We took some calls, did some traffic stops, and proactively looked for stolen vehicles to chase and secure. After the calls were cleared off the board, there wasn't much else going on. So my partner and I decided to go and visit the beat members working at the West Edmonton Mall police station. By this point, the parade chat my sergeant gave us earlier that night was the furthest thing from my mind.

As my partner and I sat there visiting the beat members, I suddenly received a call from my concerned wife. She thought someone was trying to break into our home and was currently in our backyard. I asked her to look out the window to give us the person's description. That way, we'd know what we were looking for when we arrived. But my wife was understandably scared and unable to look out the window. So I reassured her that we were on our way to check things out, and as we headed there, the beat members followed us in a separate car to give us a hand if needed.

When we arrived at my home, fresh footprints in the snow led up to our front door. However, the prints didn't track into the yard. Instead, they led from our door to the neighbour's house, where they appeared to enter the home. My wife and I lived in a cookie-cutter community in those days. Each house looked relatively the same, often resulting in mix-ups with houses when visitors arrived in our neighbourhood. Thankfully, we also had good neighbours who confirmed that their visitor had the wrong home. I reassured my wife, Colette, that things were okay and thanked the beat guys for joining us as we prepared to go our separate ways again.

Back in the patrol car, as we left the west end subdivision where my home was, I decided to head north on the highway to resume patrol of the city's west end. As I made my way north, I observed a light brown Ford F-250 truck parked on the side of the road with the cargo light on. I knew we had a rash of thefts in the city involving these particular vehicles, so I grabbed the plate number and ran it on our system as we drove by. The plate came up on our system, confirming the accurate truck model but not the correct colour. The plate I ran was registered to a *white* Ford F-250 truck, not brown. I decided to park my marked patrol car on the right shoulder of the highway to try to verify the plate of the truck that drove past us. The truck could have been a different colour for a few valid reasons.

I may have misread the plate number, or maybe the driver had bought a new truck and had yet to update the registration. Perhaps it was a plate swap, where the driver had no idea that their actual plate had been taken and replaced by this one. Maybe the vehicle was stolen, and the plate change hid that they were driving a stolen truck. I had all these scenarios playing out, mentally preparing myself to deal with whatever came my way. At the time, I did not communicate any of my thoughts to my newly graduated partner because I felt prepared and planned to stop the vehicle on my terms.

As the truck approached our marked police car, I got ready to perform a traffic stop as soon as the Ford F-250 passed us. Then something happened that I had not encountered and was not part of my thought-through scenario list. The vehicle I intended to follow as it passed us pulled alongside our patrol car and stopped beside us on the shoulder of the highway.

At this point, I felt baffled when the passenger in the truck suddenly rolled down her window and appeared to want to talk with me. As I rolled down my window, I tried to figure out why these people stopped beside me. Then, the passenger began asking for directions to Slave Lake. I could not even picture how to get there, let alone provide directions. Every intuition and feeling in my body screamed for me to get out of my police car.

In a way, policing is a funny career choice due to the uncertainty involved. Although we receive training and learn tactics to implement into our daily routine, now and then, we are faced with something new and unexpected—something we haven't considered or have even remotely prepared for. At that point, we follow our intuition and apply our experience as best we can.

At that moment, on the side of the highway, I listened to my gut instinct and exited my vehicle. It was a tight squeeze to get out of my patrol car because the truck was parked very close to my car. But, as I exited my car, I immediately saw a big black hole in the truck's steering column where there should have been an ignition switch for the keys. Right away, I knew it was a stolen truck.

I felt submerged in a massive container of molasses, and every movement I made was slow in my mind. I heard the truck's diesel engine idling and smelled the diesel exhaust in the cold December air. My head spun with scenarios as I tried to determine why these people would park a stolen truck beside a marked police car. Did they have guns in the vehicle? Were they setting up an ambush? What was their intention when they asked for directions? Were they trying to hide the fact they were driving a stolen vehicle? None of this made sense to me. Because their actions were so strange, I was highly concerned for the safety of my partner and myself. So I unholstered my issued firearm and held it at a low ready to prepare for a worst-case scenario.

I remained standing beside the truck's passenger-side mirror as I engaged the driver in a conversation. I hoped I could convince him to exit the vehicle and surrender. Unfortunately, the truck's mirror was right at my shoulder level because I am not tall at 5' 9", and this truck model is large. My conversation with the driver was short. I asked him to turn off the truck, and the driver replied, "I can't; it's stolen." I asked him to get out of the vehicle, and he responded, "I can't; my seatbelt is on." Tension was in the air as I told him he was under arrest, and I demanded him to get out of the truck using some strong language. He responded with, "I don't think so." Although my mind spun through information quickly as the scenario unfolded, what happened next felt like moving in slow motion.

The driver of the stolen truck punched the gas and cranked the steering wheel towards me. I felt the mirror jam into my shoulder and push me towards my patrol car. At that moment, I felt no fear. No actual thoughts bounced around my head, and my life didn't flash before my eyes. I knew I was in a terrible situation and would be seriously hurt or killed.

As the diesel's turbo spun up, making a whining sound that vibrated through the air, a plume of exhaust engulfed me. The rear truck tires spun about a half turn on the icy road, allowing me to react in that fraction of time. I aimed and fired at the driver as he tried to kill me by crushing me with his truck. As I pulled the trigger and shot the driver, I had no idea of the impact it would have on my life. I also had no idea that the man who pulled the trigger that night would no longer exist thirteen years later.

CHAPTER 2

Learning about Resilience

There is more to the end of the story about that fateful night on patrol and the stolen truck. After shooting the driver who led us on a twenty-eight-minute car chase, I will revisit how things transpired. But first, I think it's essential to introduce the concept of resiliency, what it means for me, and what I've learned.

I have a lot of things to be grateful for, including many from my past. The central theme of this book is resilience and one's ability to develop it. I will share how I learned to cultivate resilience and implement it into my lifestyle. Ultimately, this book centres around how I fell down a dark hole and almost lost everything but decided to reattain my resilience and learn how to climb out of that hole. What I did to acquire and implement resilience is not the only way to do it. However, by sharing the details, I hope to inspire change to improve your life regardless of where you are.

The formal definition of resiliency is the ability to bounce back to a normal state after a crisis. I mistakenly believed I was good to go once I learned about resiliency. But that is such a load of bull. I have come to understand that resilience is not a one-and-done thing. There is a massive misconception that no further work or effort is needed once we learn about resilience. As humans, we often believe that if we've bounced back from trauma nine times before, we've already learned the skills we need to cope with future traumatic experiences. We trick ourselves into believing we don't need to develop resilience because "we got this." But what about that tenth time? What happens when we don't bounce back and have done nothing to keep ourselves prepared?

We, including myself, need to work on ourselves to maintain and continually nurture resiliency. We must put in the time and effort required to establish those skills because they are imperative to overall success.

I have previously alluded to strategies I use to reinforce resilience. These strategies have helped me overcome many obstacles and consist of four steps: Awareness, Acknowledgment, Acceptance and Action. To reach a place of purpose, passion, and happiness in life, you must devote time and energy to these four concepts. But to spend time and energy, we must first understand what each of these concepts means.

Awareness: You cannot plot a new way forward unless you know where you are and where you came from. I like to compare this step to a GPS or finding a destination on Google Maps. The first thing you must do is plot the address or location of where you are currently because without this, the map application cannot plot the appropriate course for you to follow to get to your desired destination. Awareness is the starting point to recovery because it allows you to take stock of everything that has impacted you and what happened to bring you to where you are today. If we do not know what has moulded us, we cannot plot a forward course and consciously work on our resilience.

Acknowledgment: After becoming aware of where you are, at least a small piece of you must acknowledge this place. To accomplish this acknowledgment, you must recognize and understand where you are and take a moment to admit that this is your starting point.

Acceptance: As you become aware of where you are and acknowledge the starting point, you need to take a minimum of 1 percent responsibility for being where you are. Accepting this small piece of responsibility will help allow you to believe that this is where you are in life at this moment in time. Acceptance is crucial in being able to move forward toward healing and change. This step is often challenging because, as people, we tend to deflect blame or responsibility from ourselves for a variety of reasons. However, the greater the acceptance, the greater the success and change you will experience. In other words, if you can take 100 percent responsibility, you will see a 100 percent change in your situation when you get to step four.

Action: This step is likely self-explanatory, but to improve or change where you are, to find a life and live with passion and purpose or to be a little better as a person, you need to take action to initiate change. Change can be as simple as setting a goal, writing it down and working towards it.

These four concepts may seem very straightforward to understand and follow, but they can be challenging self-discovery journeys. As an example, I remember feeling a lot of guilt and shame the first time I did a reflection on my past to increase my awareness. I felt as bad about some of the things I had done as I hadn't done.

Speaking from experience, the work involved in these steps is challenging but rewarding. Every day, it requires effort because we're breaking old habits to make room for healthier ones and tearing down our walls over time. Even after all these years, this process is still a work in progress for me. I have good days and bad, but overall, I am making headway in establishing and maintaining my resiliency.

To help others understand my journey, it's prudent that I start at the beginning and provide information about where I came from and my roots. Knowing where one comes from is essential to realize how we got to where we are today.

CHAPTER 3

Growing Up

I can speak for most (if not all) of us frontline workers that we joined our specific careers to help people and positively contribute to society. We desire to leave a better legacy than when we began our jobs, or at least that is our hope.

When I started my policing career, I was a twenty-year-old man. I grew up happy, had good parents who loved me and was lucky enough to have what most people would consider a normal childhood. Nevertheless, I would take on the whole world and did not fear the future. My past created the young man I was at twenty, and my early childhood experiences moulded the traits I possessed.

Early Childhood

I was born in Newfoundland, Canada, and have Indigenous roots in my family. I am Miawupukek (an East Coast First Nations person). I am happy and proud to call myself a First Nations Indigenous person. I have very little recollection of my time on the island of Newfoundland because I was so young when we moved from there. What I feel about that place is that it is and will always be HOME for me.

I always find it difficult to answer when someone asks me where I am from. Newfoundland is what I tell them but then default back to Saskatchewan in the same breath. It is difficult to put into words, but if you're a "Newfie," you are always a "Newfie." Ask anyone you meet from there, and they will gladly, proudly, and probably boisterously tell you they are from Newfoundland. So, I often rephrase where I am from to where I grew up, Saskatchewan. But I will always be from Newfoundland.

I can almost hear the ocean waves, smell the salty sea air, and the delicious pies and fresh bread from my grandmother's kitchen when recalling my early childhood. On the flip side, I also carry a sense of loss for not learning the language and traditions of my ancestors. I also miss my family, especially my grandma. I was four years old when we moved from home, and I was sure that I would never again see any of the family that stayed behind. Thankfully, that was not the case, but I sure felt like that at four years old. I did not understand it back then, but upon reflection as an adult, I now realize that moving felt like I had my roots ripped out of the ground. As we moved from Newfoundland and travelled west, I felt like a tree with wilting leaves, transplanted in Grande Cache, Alberta—soil that felt alien to me.

Although we spent a couple of years in Grande Cache, my memory is super fuzzy about this place. I remember feeling sick a lot; I don't know whether I was. I recall my parents telling me that I was quite an active sleepwalker and liked to unlock the windows and doors in the house at night. I also remember running away from home with a friend who lived down the street. I would not characterize it as a running away event but rather more like a giant game of hide and seek with two angry, scared parents. I remember them driving along the road, calling my name as I hid on a hill behind some tall grass. It felt fun at that moment. I can tell you that when I finally showed up at home that day, I was scared because my parents were steaming mad at me. I don't recall my punishment, but it was probably significant and well deserved.

The other vivid memory I have while in Grande Cache was drinking mustard water to induce vomiting. My parents thought I had consumed leaves from the red poppies in our garden. I told them I had only eaten honeysuckles, but my mom didn't believe me, so she forced me to drink the lousy mustard water. The strategy didn't work; I didn't vomit, but I hated the smell or sight of mustard for years after that. I only recently got over my aversion to mustard in my adult years.

The Typical Canadian Kid

After a few years in Grande Cache, we moved to Hinton, Alberta, where we stayed for the next nine years. I have a lot of memories of those years in Hinton. We spent plenty of time outdoors, I went to school, and things were normal. I distinctly remember the smell of the town's pulp and paper mill; it was terrible! I made numerous tree forts, lean-tos, and ground forts in the bush behind my house. I skated on frozen lakes and ponds, was in three fistfights with no winner, and roasted hot dogs and marshmallows over open fires in the winter. I learned how to cross country and downhill ski, and I loved riding my dirt bike even though I almost killed myself twice, that I remember.

One of the most significant events I experienced and will never forget was when a dog mauled my three-year-old sister. I have very vivid pictures in my mind from that day. There was so much blood. As my sister cried, there were bubbles in the blood where her mouth and nose were. The dog bit her head, and her scalp was ripped, hanging from her ear. I felt a ton of guilt at that moment. I was responsible for watching her as we played in the front yard that day. But at eleven years old, I was more concerned with riding my bike up and down the street, so I wasn't there to protect her when the dog attacked.

I will never minimize the trauma of that event on my sister. It was horrific both physically and emotionally for her, but it was also mentally traumatic for me. It was also my first experience interacting with the police as the RCMP were present to help with my sister and find the dog's owner. As impactful as this experience was, it was then that I first learned to tuck the trauma away. The focus was on my sister and her horrific physical injuries, as it needed to be. Still, I felt that my emotions were not as important to nurture. I learned that I had to be strong for my sister regardless of what I felt inside. So, I choked it all down and tried to forget and move on. Although my sister eventually recovered from her physical injuries (seventy stitches later), the emotional and mental scars remain for us as a sad reminder of that traumatic event.

Growing up, I played hockey in the winter and golfed in the summer. I was a typical Canadian kid when it came to hockey. I loved Wayne Gretzky, Paul Coffey, Cam Neely, and Ray Bourque (all hockey players, for those who are wondering), and like most kids, I had thoughts about playing in the NHL when I grew up.

I did not start skating until I was seven years old; in hockey, seven is old. My first time on the ice, I could not stand up on skates. I repeatedly fell right at the entrance to the ice rink. I was determined to play, so I crawled to centre ice to listen to my coach. I spent the first part of the season standing, watching the play from my static position beside the bench because I could not skate.

My dad was the ultimate fanatic for my hockey playing. He always had me doing things to improve my skills, and he seemed more determined than I was to help me improve. He rented the ice for me almost every week to practice skating. Interestingly, my dad couldn't skate and still can't, but he was so determined to help that he would walk on the ice in his big winter boots. By the end of that first year of hockey, I received the award for the most improved player because I could skate at the end of the season.

As my amateur hockey career continued, my dad kept bringing me things to improve my skills. One afternoon, he brought home a steel hockey puck he made at work and a fibreglass sheet. I would spend hours standing on that fibreglass sheet with my skates, strengthening my arms and hands by passing the puck to my dad in the basement of our house. That time was about strengthening myself to pass effectively, and man, did it help. I stood on that fibreglass sheet with my skates on while shooting pucks at a net in the basement, destroying more than a few drywall sheets from all my misses.

As time went on, I improved. By my fourth year of playing hockey (and with the summer hockey camps my dad put me in), I made the AA team for my age group. I was twelve, and I specifically remember playing a hockey game in Edson where I was on the receiving end of a massive body check in the second period of that game. I had my head down, got smashed, and knocked out cold. I was out for a while, and I remember the smell of the smelling salts they used to bring me around. I was placed on the bench for that period but returned to the ice in the third period. I scored four goals that period and played amazingly well. However, I cannot remember that period of play or the drive home for about a week after that game. It was like a big black hole where memories used to be. I only know I scored those goals because my dad told me. I certainly had a concussion and probably should have seen a doctor. I also blame my limited memories of my childhood on this concussion.

Thankfully, I was fortunate to be part of some fantastic teams that won several tournaments and league championships. On the flip side, I was also part of some teams that struggled to win a single game in a season. Hockey taught me the value of hard work, being part of a team, and perseverance to never quit even when things look dim. I don't play hockey anymore because, over the years, I lost some of that passion for the game but also, I like my teeth and prefer to keep them the way they are.

Although hockey was my sport for the winter, summertime was for golf. I started my time on the golf course swinging left-handed. I was a weird kid who was right-handed with everything but shooting left-handed in hockey and golf. It was the natural way for me to swing the club, but at the age of eight or nine, Dad switched me to right-handed clubs on the advice of the golf professional at the course in Hinton. That messed up my golf game for a while. Luckily, I eventually figured out how to swing the club right-handed to hit the damn ball.

The change did not ruin my game; I could compete in multiple tournaments and play on the Junior golf night in Hinton. I was blessed to have some cool experiences and even won several junior tournaments in my local area.

As a family, we played golf all over Alberta and British Columbia. Dad and I would golf, and Mom would come along for the walk while pushing my sister in the stroller. When I was twelve, we were at a fancy course in BC, where we had a tee time booked for two. When my dad went to pay our fees, the golf pro said he wouldn't allow me to play the course, stating that I wouldn't keep the required pace for the course. Being the man he was, my dad saw a group of older women teeing off who hit their ball only eighty to one hundred yards off the tee. So, in his infinite wisdom, Dad betted the golf pro, saying that if I could hit the ball better and further than those older women, the golf pro would allow me to play the course. If I hit a bad tee shot, Dad told the golf pro we would leave and go to another course. The pro agreed to the bet, and he and my dad came out to the first tee-off box to watch me hit my drive off the tee. I had no idea that the entire round of golf hinged on my ability to outdrive the women ahead of us. I am sure my dad was confident in my ability to do this, but there was always that chance in golf that your first tee shot is a dud. So, I teed up the ball, took my stance, did the typical TV golf waggle, and swung. SMACK! The ball sailed through the air straight as an arrow and landed 170 yards down the fairway. I crushed it! It was an incredible drive. The golf pro never said a word but turned around and went back inside the pro shop while my dad and I walked down the fairway. I can only imagine how my dad felt at that moment; he was probably super proud but also very relieved that I managed to pull it off. I know he tells this story with great pride, but I have never asked him how he felt about the entire situation.

Golf is a funny game because one day, you feel you're playing like Jack Nicklaus or Tiger Woods, and the next day you golf more like Happy Gilmour when he was in the Pro-Am with

Bob Barker just before Bob knocked him out. Golf is a game I still play today, and I love being out on the course. It gives me time to be inside my head and enjoy the game, the grass, and the trees. Golf taught me to rely on my judgment, to remain calm under pressure, to have patience (oh man, did I need this), and the importance of self-confidence.

These two sports (hockey and golf) taught me some essential lessons. As I look back at when I played these sports as a kid, I have fond and disappointing memories. The key thing that stuck with me is that these sports allowed me to build that inner confidence even if I did not always show it. They provided the necessary experiences to learn how to persevere and be a part of a team. They also offered me a chance to apply the lessons learned to other situations in my life. I learned how to take direction from a coach in hockey, make decisions on my own during a golf game, and apply these skills to everything else I did. Neither professional hockey nor professional golf was in the cards for my future career. Still, it didn't matter because I had this call for service deep down. Although I had not consciously thought about becoming a police officer until years later, I realize now that the call for service was always there. I just didn't know it yet.

The Terrible Teens

We moved to southern Saskatchewan from Hinton when I was fourteen years old. We lived in Coronach, and during my first summer there, I found myself in this vast, flat, and dry place where I couldn't shake the feeling that the sky would suffocate me. There was nothing to hold up the sky, and it felt right on top of me. Even though there was such a vast open expanse of land everywhere, I felt boxed in and claustrophobic. I was used to living in the foothills of Alberta, and the sky was held up by the mountains but not here, not in Saskatchewan.

Coronach was a one-horse town with one main street with a gas station, grocery store, liquor store (doubled as the general store) and two restaurants. I liked living in Coronach and learned many life lessons during my time there.

Only twenty-four kids were in my grade, and about half were from surrounding farms. So school lessons would slow down or pause in the spring and at harvest until the seeding was done so the farm kids wouldn't fall behind in school. I thought that was great because I could play a ton of slow-pitch.

I recall hanging out with friends on the golf course one night, having a beer shortly after getting my driver's licence, when suddenly the RCMP rolled up on us. Everyone scattered in their vehicles, thinking we had successfully escaped, when the police showed up at my friend's place about an hour later, where we were all "hiding out." The officer escorted me to his patrol car to discuss what had occurred. I promptly received a twenty-four-hour licence suspension from that local RCMP officer.

I have fond memories of playing cat and mouse with our cars at night after the police were asleep at home. It was an exciting game where we would chase each other around town and try to be the first to get back to a pre-determined spot without getting caught. I also remember partying at the "trees." The "trees" were a small stretch of trees that formed an L shape (maybe thirty trees in total) in a farmer's field about twenty minutes from town. You had to know the exact location to find it, which was always great because the RCMP did not know where it was. Any time you see many trees like this, it's a big deal and a good hangout spot because, in the southern prairies, it's very flat with almost no trees anywhere. In this vast, flat expanse of land, I saw my first bonfire in which a couch provided fuel for the fire. It was party time every Thursday, Friday, and Saturday night, especially in the last few months of Grade Twelve. I have many fond memories of those experiences and adventures.

I made a close friend named Tyson, who is still my friend. Tyson is such an awesome dude and a great father to his kids. As teenagers back in the day, Tyson and I spent most of our time hanging out, having fun, and driving around the countryside. One night, we decided to grab a case of beer and go for a cruise. We headed south to some of the thrill hills, a road with peaks and valleys in a relatively flat area, and if you drove them fast enough, it felt like a roller coaster ride. This night, we saw a deer and figured it would be a good idea to chase the damn thing! Once we grew tired of chasing after the deer through the fields, we stopped for a piss, and as we were looking around the area, none of it looked familiar. Coronach had this massive power plant, and we used it as a landmark on the horizon to tell us how far south of town we were. Since Coronach was so close to the United States border, we always had to be aware of our location when we were south of town to ensure we stayed on the Canadian side of the border. We had heard rumours about the borderline being alarmed with motion sensors and that the border patrol guys used helicopters to catch border jumpers. The power plant was just a tiny spec on the horizon this night. We knew immediately that we were in the United States and that if we got caught, we would be in a pile of trouble. So, we made our way back to Canada but had to follow our tracks that weaved all over Hell's half acre to get home. Thankfully, we made it back safely and didn't see any border patrol helicopters.

Coronach was where I had my first crush, and my heart was broken (and where I probably broke a few hearts too). I bought a 1981 Honda V30 street bike and purchased my first car, a 1989 Plymouth Horizon. I put the biggest stereo and sub woofer in it that I could afford.

Coronach was also where I was responsible for looking after my little sister for three years straight. My parents worked full-time. Their shifts started before we had to make our way to school (about a ten-minute walk unless it was with my sister, which took about twenty-five minutes because she liked to doddle). Over those three years, I learned to braid her hair, make Kraft Dinner almost every lunch hour, and ensure my little sister made it to school and back home on time every day. Of course, those things were my responsibility; however, there were other things I missed out on because of it. For example, I couldn't go with my friends for lunch at the restaurant, play sports with them over the lunch hour, or hang out with them.

As a younger man, I felt I missed out on some meaningful life experiences, but now when I reflect on that time, I regard it fondly because it was special. I still had fun overall in high school and developed a healthy fear of my parents, who always expected the best from me. I momentarily rattled their trust in me when I accidentally broke a car window and initially lied about it. However, I came clean and worked off the cost of the window with help from the other friend I was with at the time. He stood up and helped me out after realizing I got caught in the lie, so thank you again for stepping up with me.

Those few years seemed to fly by before I graduated from Grade Twelve, near the top of my class. I turned down an opportunity to play Junior A hockey in Manitoba with the Portage La Prairie Bulldogs because I decided to move to Saskatoon to attend university. If there was one decision I could change, it's the one not to pursue playing Junior A hockey in Manitoba. At the time, I was too afraid to leap into billeting and playing hockey at that level. Looking back on it now, I wish I had tried. As with all things in life, we can't look back on these situations and live with regret, but we can remember them and not freeze with fear at future opportunities. All of this contributed to where I am today, and I was eager to get started on my future, excited for the adventures ahead.

Discovering My Call for Service

I enrolled in university to finish as fast as possible. To do that, I had to take all the sciences and labs. These courses were to prepare for an opportunity to apply for medicine, specifically dentistry. I had this idea in my head, reinforced over the years by my parents, that becoming a dentist was my destiny. That is what I wanted to be when I was eleven, and it stuck with my parents whenever someone asked what my future held. They always proudly responded with "Gary's going to be a dentist" whenever they talked to friends or family about my future. Being a dentist was so ingrained in my head that I ignored every other idea that came to mind. I wanted my parents to be proud of me and didn't want to disappoint them, so I went down that dentistry road. Now, I realize that all I had to do was be honest with them, and they would have supported me in whatever I decided to do.

However, there I was, attending the University of Saskatchewan in Saskatoon, living on my own for the first time, buying groceries, paying rent and bills, and having the freedom to do as I pleased. I was diligent with studying, but, somehow, regardless of how much time I put in, I could not get over 65 percent. In one of my chemistry classes, the teacher was Ukrainian and had a thick accent, so I couldn't understand a word he said when he spoke. He talked about doing the laboratories for over a week, but I had no idea what he was saying until he wrote the words on the board. I dropped the class after that day, realizing there was no way I would understand his teaching of chemistry if I couldn't understand that he was talking about the labs.

Soon into the first year of university, I realized I was overloaded and not enthusiastic about my career choice. Things were not going well. However, I learned how to shoot a great game of billiards because I spent a lot of time in the pool hall near my apartment.

I finished the first year but had to drop a couple of classes which messed up the timeline I had in my head. However, that timeline was likely unrealistic because of the changes I was dealing with. I went back to university for a second year and, after the first semester, was placed on academic probation due to my poor grade level. As time went on, I became increasingly discouraged, and my grades continued falling until I was failing. It was as if the harder I studied and pushed myself, the worse I did. The worse I did, the more I felt like a failure. I slowly realized that I was not where I was supposed to be.

I remember thinking, one Sunday afternoon, that I should drop out of university. This thought swirled in my head, but I had never quit anything before; I always finished what I started. I also knew I would need a backup plan or an idea for my life moving forward if I left school. At this point, I knew in my heart and gut that staying in university was the wrong choice. I sat with that feeling and listened to my inner voice. As I recall that moment, I recognize that this inner voice was faith, boiling over in me; faith that my future decisions would be the correct ones.

I began exploring career fairs and wrote a list of things I love doing. That list consisted of hands-on learning, driving, helping people, and wanting to do something exciting. Whenever I wrote down a possible career, I imagined myself in that job and took notes about how it made me feel. Sometimes, this imagining and working out of feelings could take a day or two. For example, one of the jobs I considered was a long-haul truck driver because I thought travelling and seeing the country would be cool. However, after a day of imagining that job—driving and sleeping in the truck every night—travelling did not seem cool. The energy wasn't there, and my gut feeling indicated that the job wouldn't be the right fit for me.

After talking to a guy dating my girlfriend's friend, I attended another career fair at the university campus. Dave was a large man, a few years older than me. The police service in Edmonton recently hired him, and he was heading to the recruit class. He recommended I check out the first responder booths, either fire, police, or emergency medical service (EMS). I took his advice and attended the fair. After having difficulty at university, I quickly ruled out EMS due to the educational requirement. The idea of more schooling seemed impossible to handle, and excitement was not there when I sat with EMS as a career choice. Next, I checked out the fire booth and sat with the fire department. This job was much harder to rule out as energy surrounded it. However, given my deep fear of fire (which developed in childhood and blossomed in my adolescence's couch-burning bonfire days), I ruled out this career prospect. I figured that a firefighter should probably NOT have a fear of fire.

My last stop at the career fair's first responders' booths was the police booth. When I sat with this career, I felt calm and enthusiastic. The energy surrounding it was so vital that I immediately knew it was my destiny. That was the call for service that I experienced. As I explored this career and the steps required to pursue it, I discovered that it includes lots of driving and helping people and is known to be an exciting career. These items were on my list of things I liked to do and wanted in a job. I also discovered that police services pay for training which was a huge bonus, and the training was hands-on, which I prefer.

While picking policing as a career, I realized I had stuck with university for my parents' sake because they wanted me to have that degree. It was more important to them than to me, so I decided to drop out of university. I realized I had something else inside me, nagging at me, and even though I picked policing, I still had no idea what my future held.

I went home, sat my parents down at the kitchen table and told them I was dropping out of university. My dad reacted quickly with this look he makes when he is pissed off. Yes, Dad, you had an *I am so pissed off right now,* look on your face. However, I diffused his anger because I had a plan. I had picked up an application for the Royal Canadian Mounted Police (RCMP) service. I showed it to them, telling them why university was not for me, but policing was. They seemed okay with my explanation and plans and were supportive of me.

After I decided to quit university and pursue a career in policing, things seemed to click into place. It seemed as if overnight, I had found my call for service and knew it was what I was meant to do. There is something to be said about having a greater purpose in life. I believe that we are all here for something bigger and more significant than ourselves. I also believe that moments in time bring us to a crossroads. Both paths may lead to the same destination, but one way is sometimes more straightforward to follow, while the other is filled with potholes that can stop us from reaching our destination. The most important thing to know is that when an opportunity comes knocking, one will experience fear, worry, and anxiety. The challenge is saying yes, stepping through that fear, and leaning into that purpose with faith that it will all work out. By moving forward, things will happen for you, although it doesn't mean you won't hear the word no a few times before you make it. Moving forward could be called perseverance, but I prefer resiliency, the ability to bounce back and move forward despite the obstacles. Let me give you an example.

After my sporting experiences and my decision to withdraw from the university, I felt good about my choice to become a police officer. I did not doubt that things were going to work out. I expected to become an RCMP officer after my first attempt at writing the entrance exam. I submitted my application and wrote the exam with that expectation in mind. I visualized myself in that RCMP uniform, working in Saskatchewan or Newfoundland. I knew I had a lot to offer the RCMP as an officer, so when I received a phone call from a recruiter, I thought I was in for sure.

However, that telephone conversation was not what I expected. The recruiter asked me several questions about my Indigenous roots. I only had basic information to offer because my family and I didn't live by those roots because of how my dad was treated back home in Newfoundland as an Indigenous male. They also asked about my appearance, and it's no secret that I seem like a regular white guy to the outside world. The recruiter continued to ask what I looked like, and when I explained to him that I had red hair, brown eyes, and fair skin, the conversation ended. It was a strange conversation. I talked about it with my mom, who said to wait and see what would happen moving forward.

About a week later, I received a letter from the RCMP on official letterhead. I eagerly opened the letter, and as I read it, my excitement faded and turned into a massive gut punch of disappointment. It said I was deferred (which isn't an outright rejection but might as well be). The reasons for the deferral were that I fell just below the exam grade required for entry as a Caucasian male. So even though my test score was high enough to qualify me for entry as an Indigenous male, I did not meet the RCMP internal requirements to be eligible as an Indigenous recruit.

To me, this deferral statement was bizarre. I am Indigenous. I have government identification and a registration number with the Government of Canada, stating that I am Indigenous and they are a direct representative of the government. The

RCMP is the face of the government in Canada—the largest police force in the country—and they said I didn't qualify as an Indigenous male. I didn't understand this. It didn't make sense. When I asked the RCMP to clarify what I needed to provide them to qualify as an Indigenous male, the RCMP stated some internal privacy policy mumbo-jumbo. I never received further clarification from them. I had this vision and dream, and I was sure this was my path, but I received a big fat NO. I was faced with a difficult obstacle.

Recently, I listened to Matthew McConaughey's audiobook called *Greenlights*, which is a great listen if you're interested. Initially, this RCMP deferral was a red light, and I could have stopped right there and given up that dream. Cue up resiliency! I realized it was merely a bump in the road, a green light to explore other options. Another way to put it is (as my mom often says) that it was a blessing in disguise. After I had dealt with feeling disappointed, I encountered a moment where I had to make another decision as to how I would move forward. I could wait for my deferral period to be over and try applying to the RCMP again, or I could find another way to make my goal happen.

CHAPTER 4

Becoming a Police Officer

I decided to explore working with other police agencies, and this decision started my journey toward being a police officer. I realized there were more police services besides the RCMP, so I decided to apply to city police services.

The first step was to list the places I would be interested in working. They consisted of the following cities: Edmonton, Calgary, Vancouver, Saskatoon, Regina, Moose Jaw, Weyburn, Ottawa, Toronto, and Halifax. In 1998, the internet was not quite at our fingertips the way it is today, so I had to call each agency and have them send me an application package in the mail. Then, I got down to business and started making phone calls. I am not sure how I found all the numbers I needed to call. I had to pay a fifty-dollar administrative fee to the agency I applied to with every application I sent. I want to take this moment to thank the bank of Mom and Dad for giving me the cash for these applications with no expectation to repay them. Thanks, guys. I love you.

As I applied to different police agencies, someone told me "NO" because some places were not hiring. Some were not interested in hiring out-of-province people, and some only wanted to hire experienced police officers. Some agencies sent me letters stating they would keep my application on file for the future. My biggest motivator for sending applications across the country was to increase the odds of getting hired. It was a shotgun approach. I didn't care about the optics of such an approach; I was determined to be employed regardless of where it was. I knew that my gut told me this is where the energy is, and this is what I wanted to do, and I was going to become a police officer come hell or high water.

As I waited to find a place to call home and a police agency to hire me, I got a job at the local tire shop. It was a place called Marv's Tire. I took that job and did not care what the pay was like, as I was grateful to have a job. I had no idea what I was doing, but I enjoyed learning to change different tires and use various tools and machines. When it came right down to it, I loved that job. I had so much fun changing car tires, and it was enjoyable when we changed the tractor and combine tires. I even remember the first time I was sent out on a service call on my own to change out a grader tire. It was exhilarating and terrifying at the same time. I almost got lost on my way out to the site of the broken-down grader. In southern Saskatchewan, there are no street signs or range road signs. You must know where to go by knowing the area; Google Maps did not exist back then.

I found the grader after about a twenty-five-minute drive. I pulled the service truck around, fired up the air compressor, and zip, zip, zip, off came the bolts. I took two long metal bars, put them under the tire, lifted them slightly, and off came the tire from the hub. I then rolled the tire up onto the road and against my truck. I muscled the new tire out onto the hydraulic ramp and used it to stand up the new tire. The key here was not to let it fall over cause if it did, it's a bitch to stand back up again. Next, I rolled the tire into the approximate area and bolt hole orientation. The grader operator lowered the axle slightly so it would be easier to lift this tire and rim back onto the grader. I put a bolt between my teeth, took those two big metal bars, propped them under the tire, lifted with all I had, and then used my shoulder to push it onto the hub. Next, I used the bars to rotate the tire ever so slightly so the holes lined up. I then took the bolt and screwed it in. SUCCESS!! With the first bolt in, the rest went in, and zip, zip, zip, I impacted them back on the grader, and I finished the job.

I thoroughly enjoyed my experience with the tire company and settled into a nice comfy routine of work and play. I had become very content to be there and was happy just sitting back and waiting for a police agency to contact me to write their entrance exam.

As the summer turned to fall, I helped with the harvest rush of service calls out in the field. Unfortunately, I accidentally turned my leather work boots into stone by spilling alkaline solutions all over them at one of the service calls. I remember the boss telling me to be careful when we put the alkaline in the tires, saying not to spill any on my boots. Well, I tried my darndest but no such luck. So I had alkaline all over my boots; by the following day, they were hard as stone and good for nothing except as a paper weight.

I continued having a great time at work and was looking forward to the winter change-over of tires for the passenger cars. As I mentioned, I was super comfortable and happy doing this type of work. I think the boss knew it too, and he could see it. One day he came over to me and told me he was laying me off because there was no work for me anymore. I was surprised and upset because I wanted to stay on and work with the company. But the boss told me that my destiny was for something more prominent, and I needed to do that and not settle down and stay in a tire shop my whole life. I disagreed with him. At that time, I took it personally that he laid me off because I had worked so hard and thought I had done an excellent job. However, looking back now, I realize he was pushing me to grow and not settle for what was easy, and his decision had nothing to do with my work ethic. I owe a lot to him because he gave me a shove when I needed it, and I thank him for seeing what was happening in those days leading up to me getting laid off from the job I had grown to love.

After getting laid off from the tire company, I was in limbo. I was without a job, not in school, and was waiting for a response from a few of the remaining ten services I had applied to across Canada. I recall having a conversation with my mom, and she asked me what I would do with the next few months. I hemmed and hawed about the right thing to do. I felt like I was wasting my time at home, and I was feeling bored and starting to have doubts about my future. I began to lose faith in the path I was sure of only a few months before. So instead of wasting my time, I decided to inquire about going to the Saskatchewan Institute of Applied Science and Technology (SIAST) to take electrical engineering technology. I had inquired about the course about three weeks before the start of the course, and they thankfully had room for me to attend. So, I enrolled in the program, and as the time came closer to its commencement, I did not feel a passion for an adventure back into school. I just wanted to be going through the hiring process for policing.

I remember sitting at home the night before the start of class, and my family and I were having supper when they asked me what I was planning to do. At that point, I still had not decided. I went to bed, and I did not choose to attend the tech school until the morning of the first class. I had to drive into Moose Jaw, a ninety-minute drive from where I was, so at 6:15 a.m., I got into my car and went to the first day of the tech program. When I got there, I was happy to learn that I knew a few people from the surrounding communities that I had partied with a bit before. I was blessed to have a great bunch of people in the program, but my heart was focused on being a police officer. During the first couple of weeks of school, I drove back and forth, deciding if I wanted to continue each day. I kept going as I waited for the invite from a police agency to write their entrance exam. Finally, the commuting became exceedingly tiresome. Winter was fast approaching, so the idea of driving ninety minutes every day across the cow path roads in Saskatchewan during the winter was not appealing to me. So, I decided to move to Moose Jaw.

The move allowed me to do other things inside that community, and one of those things was refereeing minor hockey. I had always done the refereeing thing as a teenager growing up, and I really liked doing it; it was fun for me.

As my time in Moose Jaw agonizingly progressed, I remember being at a hockey game as a linesman. While chatting with the referee, I learned he was an employee of the Royal Canadian Air Forces. He was a recruiter and tried hard to get me interested in joining the military. That was life's way of showing me another opportunity. Still, I felt uncertain when he provided me with all the military information. When I look back on this moment in time, I realize that this opportunity was being presented to me to test my resolve for becoming a police officer. First, I had to decide how important becoming a police officer was. I admit that joining the military intrigued me, and I had thought about what it would be like to join the Canadian Military. Still, I had placed my total bet on policing and was happy with that decision. However, inside of me, a fire and energy surrounding policing just wasn't there for other potential career choices, and something was nagging at me to stay the course towards my policing career and not give up.

I have to say I didn't enjoy living in Moose Jaw very much, but I made the best of it. I passed my first semester of schooling and went on to the second semester. Living in the Jaw was vanilla during that first semester of school because there was nothing extraordinary or exciting about it. Much of that had to do with me feeling like I was biding my time at school until a policing career opportunity came through. I would think about policing every chance I got. I would dream at night about it and even daydream about it during class.

During the second semester of school, I finally got a letter in the mail to attend an exam writing in Edmonton, Alberta, for the city police there. I was incredibly excited about this invitation. In my mind, my patience had finally paid off. The Edmonton City Police provided me with the opportunity to do what I had dreamed about; to become a police officer. I entered the application process with the mindset that I would do my best, and regardless of the outcome, I would learn something valuable. I felt excited and resolved that things would work out for the best whether or not I was successful. I was prepared to learn and have faith in my path.

CHAPTER 5

Some Self-Reflection

While reflecting on my life to prepare for writing this book, I recalled many memories and stories that I felt were important to share. Mainly people need to see that I am an ordinary guy doing everyday things. However, I can still learn and practise resiliency. I hope my stories will help people understand that the path to one's goals is often filled with detours. I want to show everyone that our approach is usually not straightforward and that focus and intention are essential as they shape our success on the path. They go hand in hand with perseverance and resilience. I realized many old sayings my parents told me centred around resiliency. Expressions like "you don't lose if you get knocked down; you lose if you stay down" or "keep pushing through because good things come to those who wait." These sayings could have several meanings, but they are about resilience and being aware that everything happens for a reason and at the right time.

Life provides opportunities to all of us but in different ways. Recognizing this is to be aware of what is happening and having faith that everything happens for a reason (even if we can't see or understand why) is super important. Faith or belief in the path is one of the most critical and nerve-racking things to get your head around. That is especially true when you are older and more experienced, as we tend to act and behave more logically based on our life experiences. We may face a moment or a situation that appears to be negative or has some negative impact on our lives. When this happens, because it will happen, we must accept that we cannot go through life without facing some hardships, receiving an answer of NO, and failing at some things. However, we must strive to see the opportunity in these situations. When we are young, it's easy to find a different path as we are more pliable and flexible inside of the adversity we face. It takes faith, belief, and the ability to use our awareness to stay the course or see the alternate path we should be taking instead. When things get complicated, and we experience a failure or disappointment, it's an opportunity for our character to evolve and learn how to be resilient and persevere.

Part of my awareness in my journey to becoming a police officer was that I had set my mind to something I wanted, and nothing would take that away from me. The amount of effort or obstacles I might face didn't matter because my goal was clear. Even when other opportunities presented themselves, I leaned into faith not to stray from my path, which filled me with a sense of calm and assurance.

My policing career path has taken me into places I was unprepared for, even with all the training I received. The mental and emotional strain of being a police officer, or any first responder, is challenging for people outside of the profession to understand fully. I am not suggesting that people cannot comprehend that first responders go through stress and strain. However, I believe it's hard for those who aren't in the profession to fully grasp and understand what we feel because of what we see. I would argue that even with careful preparation, things may still be difficult to process when faced with the actual situation.

Sometimes it's hard for people to separate an individual from their career, and they forget that this individual leads another life outside their job. Some people are unsympathetic towards individuals because of their career choice. They may say, "they knew what they signed up for when they chose that career," or "it's part of their job." But the most significant piece of awareness is those first responders are human too, and things will affect us regardless of our preparation.

I have come to accept that just because I am a police officer doesn't mean I have immunity to feelings and emotions that we all experience as humans. Just because I put on a uniform and a Kevlar vest doesn't mean I am emotionally bulletproof. Like every other human on this planet, I poop, pee, bleed, cry, ugly cry, feel happy, get aroused, feel sad and get angry. I have crappy days, get down on myself and act defensively. I feel depressed, worthless, fantastic, invincible and experience pretty much every other situational emotion that one can experience. The uniform I must wear does nothing to make me immune to my experiences. The uniform is just fabric made from polyester and wool, which is itchy and unflattering.

One of the more challenging aspects of this career choice is that first responders experience an accumulation of stress. That is because we are subjected to this stress daily, and as it builds, it starts to change us and weigh us down. When the pressure begins, we usually find ways to cope with keeping ourselves functioning. But, as the stress increases, it starts to pile up, and our coping strategies begin to fail. As we struggle to navigate these emotional pressures, our behaviours change. Emotions get brought home from work, and we try to protect those closest to us by keeping things bottled up inside. We think to ourselves, no one wants to hear about that fatal car crash I dealt with at lunch where somebody killed a child, so I'll just say nothing and pretend it didn't happen. Then one day, when you least expect it, BANG! That final straw breaks the proverbial camel's back, and you crash hard.

That was the case with the shooting I was involved with on patrol that particular night. The shooting was the tip of the iceberg that sank my ship. Before that, I was like the Titanic, steaming ahead as fast and carelessly as I could through the iceberg-riddled ocean. I ignored the signs. I had lost my ability to be aware. The water around me was calm, so I pushed on with the same arrogance as Captain Edward Smith because, just like the Titanic, I felt unsinkable in my mind. Most of my accumulated stress was under the water, lurking like that iceberg and silently building throughout the years of my attended calls. Not only was it work stress that built up, but personal stress had built up for me, and I had no idea it was even building until it was too late. The disaster was coming, and it was only a matter of time before I ran my ship into the underbelly of that iceberg. Afterwards, I would find myself clinging to pieces of the wreckage. I was barely keeping my head above water, trying not to freeze to death in the middle of my Atlantic Ocean like the passengers aboard the Titanic on that fateful night in 1912.

CHAPTER 6

Constable Gary Benoit

The year was 1999, and the New York Yankees won the World Series, the Denver Broncos were Super Bowl champs, and the Dallas Stars won the Stanley Cup for the first time in franchise history. The "Great One" Wayne Gretzky played his final professional hockey game, and I was beginning my career in law enforcement.

When the City of Edmonton Police Service hired me, I was twenty years old and thought I had the world by the tail. I entered the recruiting class with thirty amazing people with more life experience than I had. I decided that my best way through all this was to blend in. I planned to be somewhere in the middle of the pack because I knew that it ultimately didn't matter if you were at the top or the bottom of the class if you made it through and that when this was all over, people still called you Constable. So, with that plan in mind, I stayed somewhere in the middle as I tried to take it all in. I did not say much unless someone asked, and I did my best to support those around me.

During the early weeks of recruit class, I experienced an unexpected traumatic event that I chose not to deal with. I lost my grandfather in week seven of my training. I remember getting the call at my one-bedroom apartment after a long day of training and thinking there was no way I could go to the funeral. I had firearm training the next day, which I was sure I wouldn't be allowed to miss; plus, I liked those training days because I was a decent shot. But the next day, as we trained with our firearms, I messed up and missed the targets. My head was not in it. One of the firearms trainers approached me, pulled me aside, and chatted with me. When I told him about my grandfather's passing, he was understanding. It was the human side of my trainer that I had not seen since the start of training. He then must have spoken to his chain of command because the next day, somebody told me that the police service, the police association, and my classmates had all chipped in to fly me down to Newfoundland to attend my grandfather's funeral. I was at a loss for words and exceedingly grateful for this gift. It meant more to me than I could say, but I don't think I could communicate how important this was for me. I did bring back a big cooler full of fresh fish that I gave to the class as a thank you. However, the loss of my grandfather was more impactful than I realized, and that is when the slow accumulation of stress began.

I use the word stress here and will couple it with an often misunderstood term: grief. I should expand on this point for a moment. As a society, we link grief and the feeling of sorrow to just the loss of a person. We say things when faced with someone grieving that are not always helpful. Often, we say something like, "you have to be strong for your family," or "things will get better with time because time heals all wounds." We might say, "just keep busy, and if you focus on doing things, the pain will subside," or "your grandfather would not want you to quit what you're doing, so you have to keep at it." None of these statements make the feeling go away. Keeping busy pushes the feelings down, and they never get resolved. Believing in these "myths" causes additional stress on ourselves. When we express these statements to someone grieving, we feel less awkward and better about ourselves, but we're not helping the griever. I was privy to most of those statements, which added to my stress backpack because I had unresolved grief. I began to carry that around even before taking calls for service.

Essentially, I was experiencing the loss of my grandfather, and I could not process any of this. However, I was told I needed to be strong in honour of my grandfather and push through my training because he would have wanted me to. At this point, I began subconsciously making small boxes in my mind to compartmentalize the things that bothered me. I did my best to move on and forget those moments and events or how they made me feel.

As a twenty-one-year-old man, I successfully completed the first part of my training. After that, I began the field training component for my policing career in South Division in Edmonton. Finally, my dream of becoming a police officer was coming true, and I was on cloud nine and couldn't be happier. I remember my first moments in the patrol car as I orientated to the equipment and the Mobile Data Terminal (MDT). The memory of the MDT is something that I cherish to this day. That little computer had a tiny six-inch screen with orange writing and MS DOS-style programming. The computer used keystrokes to perform searches, making this god-awful beep when it received a message or a result. As I was trying to figure out the MDT, someone began talking to us through the radio. However, I had no idea what they said because my "radio ears" were still too new and inexperienced to make out actual words. Then, suddenly, we were off lights on and flying down the street.

We raced to my first call for service, a 10-13. That is the police code for when an officer is in trouble and needs assistance immediately. We headed into the Millwoods community, and I was still learning the city's layout, so I was just along for the ride. When we arrived at the call, it was absolute chaos. There were at least seventy-five people in the parking lot of this neighbourhood pub. The crowd surrounded two police officers struggling to arrest these two out-of-control guys. I remember sitting in the vehicle as we pulled up, and I had no idea what

I was supposed to do. My field trainer said, "Let's get in there and help those two!" So, I waded into the crowd pushing my way past them as they yelled at us. To be honest, I had tunnel vision and have very little recollection of the people in the crowd. But I remember the two guys fighting with the other police members in the middle. They were large guys, drunk, and appeared to be superhuman. I grabbed one of the guy's arms, and he lifted me clear up off the ground with a straight arm like he was doing a shoulder raise exercise in the gym.

Somebody hit that guy square in the junk, and he didn't flinch! Instead, he said something like, "Jesus, that smarts b'y," in a Newfie accent. I felt very inadequate at that moment, and I was terrified. Then someone else unleashed the pepper spray, and I received a healthy dose as well as the bad guys. Thankfully, we could wrestle the guys down to the ground and place them in cuffs, but I was coughing like crazy, couldn't see anything, and my skin was burning like it was on fire. My adrenaline was through the roof. I desperately needed water to get the pepper spray off my skin and out of my eyes. As I got up after the guys were arrested, an officer from another squad patted me on the shoulder and said, "Welcome to patrol, rookie."

That was my first call and experience as a sworn police officer. I honestly felt like I was way out of my element and filled with excitement, energy, and adrenaline. At the same time, fear, anxiety, pressure, and uncertainty tempered these exciting emotions. I felt so much, so fast that it was difficult to process everything, and never had I, in my short life, felt anything like that experience. We continued to take calls after that, but I have no memory of the rest of that shift. However, a few things lingered from that first call, which prompted me to make some changes. After experiencing that terrifying feeling of helplessness as they hoisted me up into the air against my will, I told myself I would never again be the slim 160 lbs I was. I felt like I could not do my job and did not want to feel that way again. As a result, I started to eat bigger meals and work out more. Unfortunately, that call also seemed to set the tone for my whole career as I faced high-priority calls and stressful situations, one after another.

Being twenty-one years old, I had no idea what I was supposed to do with the feelings I was experiencing. I did not want to tell anyone what I felt because I did not want to look weak in front of my squad, and I wished to fit in. So instead of dealing with my feelings, I pushed them back and buried them deep within my subconscious. At that time in policing, no one discussed Post Traumatic Stress Disorder (PTSD), and it was not something anyone admitted to having. It was viewed as a weakness to have those feelings or anxieties. To be a good cop, you had to be tough and put those things out of your mind. The police force expected you to suck that stuff up and move on to the next call, rewarding yourself with a drink or two to blow off the steam after your shift. So, that's what I did.

CHAPTER 7

The Cracks Start to Form

As I mentioned before, part of the training to become a police officer involves field training, where you're assigned a specific Field Training Officer (FTO) to teach you the ropes. My FTO was an excellent trainer and an even better man. He treated me with respect and was very reasonable when I made mistakes, and man, did I make mistakes. I even ran over his metal clipboard (the tin) as I pulled the patrol car up to the front of the station to pick him up at the beginning of a shift.

I should explain the significance of the tin. It was a piece of equipment that doubled as a platform for writing tickets or court documents. It also held every release document and attachment for ongoing investigative files. Back then, we hand-wrote everything, so losing that or damaging the tin and its contents was a big deal. Unfortunately, the day I ran my FTO's tin over, we didn't realize I did it. When my FTO couldn't find his tin in the car, we returned to the station. All the paperwork scattered across the parking lot; the tin flattened like a pancake on the ground. I felt so embarrassed and terrible about the situation, but my FTO was good to me and showed me incredible grace and patience.

Part of the FTO's responsibilities is to take the recruit to various calls for service. That helps expose recruits to as many situations as possible to help prepare them for their careers. As my FTO fulfilled his duties, he took me to my first sudden-death service call. A teenager committed suicide in his parent's backyard using his father's shotgun. I will never be able to erase that scene from my memory. If you are a first responder reading this, you know exactly what I mean. I not only have the images permanently burned into my head, but when I think about that moment, I still remember the smell of gun powder and the scent of blood in the air.

I also remember the overwhelming grief the family experienced and how powerless I felt to help them. But we were there to do a job. The family counted on us to do something—anything— to help them process the next steps of that horrific tragedy. I had to push aside all the overwhelming emotions at that time. I had to focus on my job, search for a suicide note, and investigate the death and storage of the firearm. I felt completely numb. I don't remember what I said to the family, but it likely wasn't what I felt for them. The kid was only sixteen and from a good home with parents and a sibling who loved him. It was a heartbreaking situation. Not experienced enough to hide them, I am sure I wore my emotions on my face. However, when my FTO asked if I was doing okay, I replied, "Yep, all good." Those words "I'm good" became my standard response to most situations from that point on.

As my field training progressed, some things became routine, and I started to feel like I was getting the hang of things. But now and then, we'd get a call that would totally throw me for a loop. I remember working first watch one morning, thinking how beautiful the sky looked with a fantastic sunrise. The air was calm and had that fresh, crisp smell of summer mornings around Edmonton. Suddenly, this peaceful, serene moment vanished as we responded to a 911 call from a woman screaming that someone was killing her. We quickly arrived at an apartment complex. Exiting our patrol car, we could hear a woman screaming as somebody chased her. We then observed a woman running on the sidewalk in the complex. She was wearing only her underwear and bleeding heavily from the skin hanging on her arms and legs, wounds she received from being sliced with a knife. As she ran to me, I directed her to the ambulance on the roadway because I had to turn my attention to the man chasing her. He held a large, bloodied kitchen knife and looked enraged. Facing my first lethal threat encounter, I drew my firearm and started yelling at the man to get him to drop the knife. I could tell he was looking right through me to the woman he was so mad at and intent on harming further. I pointed my gun directly at him, but he continued to walk toward me, refusing to listen to my verbal instructions.

In training, we learned that anyone with a knife should not get within twenty-one feet of you. That is because that person could still harm you even after being shot if they are within that distance. My only frame of reference was my training, so I relied on that and my intuition in this situation. I continued to yell at the man and was yelling the same thing repeatedly, "Drop the knife!!" The man was now within those critical twenty-one feet of me. I glanced down and saw a crack in the sidewalk just a few feet in front of this man, and I decided that if he touched that crack, I would shoot him. Next, I yelled at the man that I would shoot him if he took three more steps in my direction. As I repeated that statement a second time, he took two more steps toward me and stopped one foot shy of that crack in the sidewalk. He dropped the knife, and I was able to prone him on the ground to take him into custody without further incident.

I can say with certainty that the crack in the sidewalk was only ten feet from where I was standing before the man finally complied and dropped the knife. My adrenaline was through the roof, and my heart felt like it would beat right through my chest. Just writing about that situation, my adrenaline increases, and my heart rate elevates. At that moment, I learned to follow my intuition and use my training as that overarching guide because I would have failed if this had been a training exercise. But, as my FTO told me, training and real life are different. Things never unfold the same way in a controlled environment as in real life; therefore, my perception and reaction to a situation will be influenced by what is happening. Those decisions will be mine to make and mine to own as an officer.

I look back on that situation and wonder why I didn't pull the trigger at the twenty-foot mark. I believe I didn't because the man had slowed down (he was no longer running in my direction). There was sufficient distance between him and the woman he intended to harm. I also didn't believe the man was a threat to me precisely because it was clear his focus was solely on his female victim. So, I waited beyond the threshold of my safety to spare this man from my firearm's possible fatal injury, and thankfully, it worked out OK that time. After this event, I felt great that we could help the woman who, likely, would have been killed by the man chasing after her. However, I was unprepared for the adrenaline dump and the anxiety-riddled second-guessing I would experience afterward.

Second-guessing your decisions can sometimes feel akin to emotional torture. You agonize over the details, play out the scenario of different choices in your mind and constantly wonder about the elusive "what ifs?" After experiencing my first lethal threat encounter, I began having vivid dreams about these scenarios. In some dreams, I was successful and survived; in others, I got shot and floated over my body as the dream continued. I did not think the dreams were a problem or even a symptom of the emotional trauma I experienced. But I realize now that my stress was starting to build.

It's essential to take a step back here and explain that recounting these experiences and memories has been difficult for me. This stage in the healing process is also time-consuming because I had to go back into my memory, go over these events and try to find the good in each one. Then I had to be okay with what happened and find some gratitude for it. There is a slight danger in going over each event in this type of detail. The first time I did this exercise, I hit the basics of each event, not the details. Then, as I developed a stronger foundation and a better platform for resiliency, I could look deeper at each event. It took baby steps for each one. Also, each event is unique. For some, I could look back at them and analyze and resolve things quickly, while some events took a long time to sort out. This process was therapeutic for me. Talking about all these events and going over each one was helpful. However, the flip side of reliving these events was not always beneficial because it surfaced all these traumas I had lived through. However, this step was necessary, and only by confronting these problematic memories was I able to find the lessons I had learned and have gratitude for them. That was the most valuable part. Gratitude is one of the most significant things to use to build resilience. That is what the awareness and acknowledging steps did for me. I could bring what was in my subconscious into the conscious, and by doing this, I could face the feelings head-on.

CHAPTER 8

Life and Work

Life hurried on, and as I moved forward in my policing career, I continued to move onwards in my personal life. I finished my field training and officially became a police officer. I also met a woman, fell in love, and got married. Things seemed great on the surface, but perfection was far from reality. I hurried into a marriage I was not ready for, and I struggled to juggle my personal life against the demands of my career. As work became busier and more intense, I slowly distanced myself from my parents, sister, and friends and distanced myself from my marriage. I put all my energy into my policing career because it was a dream that I fought hard to make a reality.

However, devoting all my energy to my job meant I could not focus much time on anything else. Regularly missing family holidays (Thanksgiving, Christmas and Easter) or birthdays and anniversaries were not something my wife would accept for twenty-five years. As time went on, things deteriorated, and I fell into the trap of blaming others. I deflected blame for my struggles because it was easier to do that instead of taking responsibility for my actions.

As my personal life strained, I also compartmentalized my policing experiences, especially those experiences that impacted me emotionally. I don't remember the exact order of these events, but there were four significant situations I experienced while working in Edmonton, South Division, that added to my baggage.

One instance was a collision on Highway 2 just inside the Edmonton City Limits in the highway's northbound lanes. A semi-truck struck a male pedestrian, and my partner and I were first on the scene. I remember walking towards the victim lying in the middle of the roadway, piled up with his limbs facing every direction except for how they should have. He had no recognizable facial features. It was an awful sight, and in my head, I tried to delete that image by replacing it with the only thing that made sense to me: one of those gory rubber Halloween masks. The problem with doing that was every time I saw a gory Halloween mask on a shelf somewhere, I thought about that scene on the highway, and the blood and brain matter scattered everywhere. So that was a mistake. Instead of improving the situation, I made it far worse. That is when I learned to never, and I mean never, make those internal connections with my service calls to things around me or things in everyday life. After this traumatic experience, I disassociated and separated my calls for service from any similarities in regular life. As a result, this scene doesn't bother me nearly as much as before. I can go Halloween shopping, and rarely am I reminded about this event anymore.

The following situation was when my partner and I attended a break and enter-in-progress where three males were inside a residence armed with guns. My partner and I were first on the scene and contained the home as best we could. A male came out of the house, and I directed him to the ground and arrested him with the assistance of our staff sergeant. The male had a loaded handgun on him at the time of his arrest, and we apprehended the other two suspects using a dog track. It was an exciting call and one that my partner and I were both proud of. But after some reflection, we realized that we were fortunate that the two other armed suspects fled out the back and did not come around the house and ambush us. After that call, this realization played with my head, causing my lethal threat encounter dreams to intensify for a while. I also began to get used to the adrenaline rush and excitement that comes with a call like that. Having that type of rush becomes addictive, and you want more of it because everything becomes more vibrant and apparent. But seeking out that rush means facing situations that cause chronic stress, adding to that emotional backpack's weight.

Another circumstance was an armed robbery that my partner and I responded to that we didn't know was an armed robbery until we arrived out in front of the business. This call came in close to quitting time, and because of that, complacency kicked in. I assumed this was a nothing 911 call because dispatch relayed that nothing was said or heard on the call. While arriving at that call, I was just so ready to finish my shift that I was mentally already at home, tucked into my bed. When we arrived on the scene, my partner was observant enough to smack me back into reality. He directed my attention to the suspect, pointing a gun at a civilian's head as a robbery unfolded at the bar. As we positioned ourselves outside the bar, a second suspect exited the front doors. Upon seeing the police presence, he surrendered to us. While we arrested him, we found a loaded gun in his pocket and learned that there were ten hostages duct-taped in the bathroom. There was one suspect still inside, armed with a handgun, and only my partner and I were on the scene for the moment. We set up containment, and I had accidentally left my patrol car running and unlocked, which gave the suspect a method of escape. The commander then had my rear tires shot out so the car would be somewhat disabled if the suspect tried to flee in my patrol car. Although the suspect ended up fleeing out a rear exit of the bar during the process of our initial containment setup, the result was good, and we were able to save all ten hostages. This call may not seem like one that would add to the mental baggage I was carrying, but a lot of second-guessing occurred. I had felt ashamed, embarrassed, and guilty for parking my car like that and leaving it running. I repeatedly played that scenario in my head, swearing to myself that I would never make that same mistake again. That call was full of teaching moments, and although I was proud of our efforts and that we saved ten innocent people from harm, I was bothered by my mistake.

I find the things that seem to stick with us and get under our skin very interesting. I am always trying to learn more about myself, and through the years, I have come to understand that I always wanted to be one of the best at everything I was doing. But as much as it was hard to admit, I can be somewhat easily discouraged. Looking back at my life, it was not my nature to be the centre of attention. I was always shy and quiet. Those traits caused me to internalize many things and not verbalize what was bothering me. This method of coping meant I spent a lot of time in my head. All this internalization fuelled those dreams that I continued to have. Some dreams were about mistakes I made; some were about the achievements of catching the "bad guy," and others were about lethal encounters.

The last situation that occurred before I transferred out of the South Side Division really bothered me. It was a 911 call where a young woman was on a high-level bridge wanting to commit suicide. Upon our arrival, we learned that the woman had run down to the river's edge, so that's where we headed to search for her. As we combed through the trees and bushes along the river, someone told us they saw her back up on the bridge. We started to run up the steep embankment through the trees, and by the time I got to the top, I was spent. We saw the woman begin running towards the middle of the bridge over the river, and we began running after her. She dropped her purse, shoes, and coat as she ran. I started picking these items up as I was running after her because I was the third officer in the line behind my partner. As we got closer, she climbed onto the railing, sat for a split second, then dropped to a hang. She looked back at us as we closed in, and my partner was within arms reach of her when she let go. From my vantage point, I could see her face, which was pretty, resolved, and free of fear. She fell like a leaf from a tree, not making a sound. In my mind, everything was dead quiet as she fell through the air. It appeared to be so peaceful until she hit the water. That was the loudest sound I had ever heard, and it startled me back to the chaos surrounding us. A distraught husband screamed, traffic sped by, and other bystanders stood around in disbelief. I stood at the railing with all her stuff in my hands as she floated down the river. There were other police members on the shoreline, and I tried to give updates on her location so we could recover her and maybe still save her, but she was never found. This event filled me with so much guilt and sadness. I felt so bad about not being able to catch her. I was angry at myself for not being in better shape so that I could have run after her faster, and I was mad about my belt and boots being so heavy.

I never told anyone what I was feeling. Instead, I said things like, "this is just the crappy part of the job," or "you can't save everyone," and "if we had saved her that day, she probably would have just done it another day." All logical statements are used as a coping mechanism because, heaven forbid, I tell anyone what I felt. When people asked how I was doing, I always replied, "I'm good," or "I am fine, thanks for asking." I even convinced myself that I was superb at compartmentalizing and separating what I felt with my day-to-day activities away from the job. I felt like things were going okay, but my world was crumbling. I was unable to communicate my feelings, and I felt isolated.

My marriage was failing, and although we continued to try and fix things, the shine of being married to a police officer had worn off for my wife. One moment stuck out to me, and that was when my wife told me that she wanted me to return to school and become a lawyer. I explained how that would not happen, so she gave me an ultimatum that I either quit policing or she would leave me. This conversation happened just shy of our first-year wedding anniversary, and I told her that there was no way I was ever quitting policing. I had worked too hard to achieve this dream, and I wouldn't just let it go. The lines were drawn in the sand, and we were on a crash course we could not escape.

CHAPTER 9

Hard Decisions

In early 2002, I requested a transfer to West Division to broaden my policing career further. That was a good move for me as I felt refreshed to be in a new squad and new division. The transfer also provided a welcome distraction from what was happening at home in my personal life. Things were bad at home, but things were going great at work. I was having fun, learning new skills, and making new friends. However, my nights were restless because of my dreams. I still had those vivid dreams, and they became an almost every night thing. As they became more consistent, a couple of them began reoccurring repeatedly.

Three dreams repeated themselves. The first dream was when I was involved in a call and got shot, and I would hover over my body as paramedics worked on me. That dream always ended with me waking up right in the middle of being transported to the hospital. The second was a dream where I got shot but could return fire and call for help. That one always ended with me surviving and going back to work. The third dream was one where I was involved in a lethal encounter, and no matter what, I could not get my gun out of the holster; even if I did, the gun would not fire. The locations of these dreams and the suspects were always just a blur. I kept brushing the dreams off and tried my best to forget them. I even told myself they were a good thing as I was mentally preparing for my job while I slept, which sounds ridiculous now that I say that aloud.

By this point, things had eroded even further at home, stressing me out about all the crap. I only interacted with my friends while I was at work and often chatted about some of the stuff happening at home, which was more of a vent session. I am sure my squad was getting tired of the venting sessions. I remember one day when I was talking with one of my squadmates; he said something to me that was incredibly honest. I am unsure if I ever thanked him for being so candid, but he asked me a question. He asked, "If things are so bad at home, why don't you just leave her?" It was like a lightbulb went off in my head. I had no answer for such a straightforward question, but he was right. My wife and I were only making each other miserable. Thankfully, we hadn't yet brought kids into the mess. I realized that leaving now would be the best for both of us and that we would be happier going our separate ways in the long run.

I packed up and left, taking only my clothes, guitar, snowboard, golf clubs, hockey equipment and some toiletries. This decision was so liberating that it felt like I had removed 500 pounds from my shoulders. The divorce eliminated much stress from my mind. Now, arguments and anxiety did not fill my time outside of work. After moving out, I felt lighter. I reconnected with my family and spent more time out with my friends. Although the journey wasn't easy, it was necessary and opened new doors for me, and I am forever thankful.

As I reflect on where I am now and acknowledge those first few years in policing, I remember the power of deciding. Over the last few years, I have been working with a life coach, and through that process, I have been able to re-wire my brain and how I think about things. My coach, Stacey Berger, the founder of Ever-Expanding Coaching, taught me about a power that exists for all of us but is rarely understood or used to its fullest potential. That is the power of *making a decision*, how the universe works when we make decisions, and what happens when we stay frozen in indecision.

Jack Canfield is the author of *Chicken Soup for the Soul*, and he talks about the power that lies with making decisions. He says that when you make decisions quickly, things start to move and rearrange for you as you decide. Avoiding the pitfalls of indecision by actively making a choice allows things to improve because we remove the worry, doubt, and anxiety around that decision. As we evaluate what we want and how we want to live, there comes a time to decide what we will do to make those desires a reality. There is unbelievable power inside those decisions. Too often, we stay in the moment of indecision. We sit there sometimes due to the fear and uncertainty surrounding the decisions that we must make. Or we don't follow through with deciding because we don't want to be uncomfortable. As human beings, we like to be comfortable because it makes us feel secure. We will even stay in a comfortable and familiar environment, even if that environment is toxic and harmful to our mental health. What is that adage, "Better the devil you know than the devil you don't."

When faced with making a change or being presented with an incredible opportunity, it's normal to be afraid or uncertain. Remember to have faith if you find yourself at the edge of a decision and that possibly crippling fear is there. Although it may not seem like it now, I promise you that incredible things are on the other side of your worst fears. Herein lies the power of deciding. It's like taking a leap of faith by stepping through that fear; when you do, the Universe reveals remarkable things. I can honestly say that I have had the best things happen every time I have fought off the fear and decided. For example, after making the scary, difficult decision to leave one relationship, I met the most fantastic woman, Colette. I am now lucky to call her my wife. In a perfect world, we would be able to balance this incredible power of prompt decision-making in all facets of our life, but this is not an ideal world! Although I had gained a significant level of self-awareness to move through my life challenges, I continued to struggle with that awareness in my policing career. Unfortunately, it would take many years later and an officer-involved shooting until I learned to make changes in my life again.

CHAPTER 10

The Bumpy Road Ahead

During my time in West Division, I grew and had the opportunity to work with some fantastic people. I am so grateful to the people I worked beside, in the patrol car and within the squads. I learned to be an excellent patrol officer over the next few years. I honed my proactive and investigative skills. I found that I had a knack for finding stolen cars, and those usually ended up in a car chase full of adrenaline, excitement, and danger. Unfortunately, the time in West Division seems compressed and fast, with my memory for those years being very blurry and spotty. I blame that on the stress I was under and that I had not dealt with the post-traumatic stress I had experienced previously.

One specific impactful event during my earlier years in West Division was when my partner and I assisted two other officers with arresting a male who damaged the inside of a Money Mart. The suspect was dishevelled, not wearing any shoes, and believed high on methamphetamine. Upon our arrival, we tried to arrest the male suspect, but he immediately resisted. We eventually got him on the ground in an attempt to put him in handcuffs, but he began to spit at us. So, I stuck my left hand over his mouth to shield us from his spit in reaction to him spitting. Well, that was a colossal mistake! After placing my hand by the suspect's mouth, he bit down on my ring finger with a vice-like grip. Everything we tried to get him to stop biting me was to no avail as the suspect continued biting harder. Finally, I pulled out my pepper spray and emptied the can into his nose, throat, and face. It did not help one iota as he continued to crunch down on my finger. My partner tried some tactical body and head strikes, which also did nothing. It was like the suspect possessed superhuman strength, and the pain in my caught finger was nearly unbearable. By this point, I was scared that he would bite right through my glove and take off my finger. I was in a panic and desperate, so I reached for my partner's baton because I could not reach mine, and my thoughts were that I would probably have to break the guy's teeth to free myself. But at that moment, the suspect coughed, and I freed myself from his grip with my finger still attached. We took him to the hospital, and I had my finger inspected.

The doctor told me I still had a finger only because I wore my Kevlar-lined gloves. I am reminded every day about the impact of this event because I still, to this day, have no feeling in my ring finger between my knuckles. When I put on my wedding ring, it reminds me to be grateful to have this finger still.

As time went on, I transferred briefly to Traffic Section on my supervisor's advice to explore some other areas of police work. Although I liked all the members in Traffic (they were indeed a fantastic bunch), I did not like the work as much as I enjoyed patrol. So I decided to transfer back into patrol. As luck would have it, I was able to transfer into patrol back at my old stomping grounds of West Division. After my brief experience in Traffic Section, I decided to remain in patrol moving forward because patrol work was what I loved doing best. I enjoyed the randomness of our calls, the uncertainty of what we might face and the camaraderie between my squadmates. I decided to do what I wanted for myself and not for anyone else, which is important.

Being back in West Division felt like home, and I got assigned to West Squad 4 in the spring of 2006. I was working for an exceptional sergeant whom I thoroughly respected. He was good at what he did and created a space for us officers to develop within our careers. Around that same time, Colette and I joyfully welcomed the arrival of our son. Although I see our son's arrival as a blessing, the situation was far from blissful. Having a child significantly added to the stress levels I was experiencing. Colette and I were not married when our son arrived, but we lived together. Colette was super patient with me and most of my shortcomings, but we were ill-prepared for a new baby. Our son was delightful in many ways, but boy was he fussy! He was the first grandchild for both of our families, and in their excitement, the grandparents wanted to come and visit us to see the little guy.

With permission from my lovely wife, I openly share that Colette suffers from obsessive-compulsive disorder (OCD). Nothing overt or debilitating, but Colette likes things to be tidy, and she needs to entertain or host when people stay at our house. We lived in an 1100 square foot, two-storey home, which meant 550 square feet per level. A.K.A. was not very big. With our families living outside Alberta, we always hosted when anyone came to see us in Edmonton. That was fine and dandy as we enjoy hosting and catching up with friends and family. But when you throw a newborn baby into the mix and post-delivery recovery, our house looked more like a closet than a home.

My excited parents arrived in Edmonton with all the anticipation of first-time grandparents. They came to stay with Colette and me to welcome our new bundle of constant-crying joy, but with the extra people in that small space, there was nowhere to go to get some private time. Colette was still recovering from giving birth, and our new baby boy cried twenty-two hours a day. Neither of us was sleeping, and we struggled greatly with our son. During this difficult and stressful time, the constant company in our home started to take a hard toll on my wife and me. I could tell that Colette needed space to relax and not feel like she was in "hosting" mode. We also required privacy to adjust to this entirely new experience. I was grumpy; hell, we were all cranky. I felt that plastering on a fake smile to my parents and carrying on a conversation wasn't favouring anyone. All I wanted to do was close my eyes on my sofa and sleep for an hour because it was the first time my son had stopped crying that day. So, I decided to have a challenging and awkward conversation with my parents. I asked them how long they intended to stay at our place and if they would be willing to stay in a hotel for Colette's comfort during their visit.

I am unsure how I communicated my concerns (our baby not sleeping, Colette needing her space and our mental and physical exhaustion) to my parents. Still, I was probably not as articulate as I should have been. The conversation upset my mother, and although my dad was trying to be good to me about it all, he also needed to support my mom. I tried like hell to explain to my parents what was going on and that I meant no offence, but it was to no avail. My parents decided not to stay in a hotel, but instead, they left Edmonton to go home back to Saskatchewan. That was the most challenging moment in my relationship with my parents. One decision forever changed our relationship moving forward. From that moment on, I have felt like they stopped treating me like a son, and our future visits have sometimes felt exceedingly tough and awkward, like walking on eggshells. I have tried to apologize several times for that conversation and what I said or how I made them feel, but I can't erase the past. If I could do it over, I would have taken some more time to articulate my concerns better. I was trying to do what was best for Colette and me while supporting my wife in her moment of need. I never intended to make my parents feel like we did not want them in our home. Instead, I wanted them to understand that we needed some space to adjust to this new and stressful situation.

I have played that moment repeatedly in my mind, and I have concluded that at that moment, I was doing what was best for Colette and me. I do not regret asking for that space because I was being honest and communicating a problem to my parents instead of pretending we were okay. I can also accept and acknowledge that I unintentionally hurt my parents at that moment, and I take responsibility for that. I also understand that when they came to stay at our home to visit their first grandchild, they came over out of love and support for Colette and me. Sometimes miscommunications happen, and we inadvertently hurt those we love. The one thing I regret (for both my parents and my son's sake) is that my parents missed out on some notable moments in my son's life. If we didn't have that difficult strain in our relationship all those years ago, maybe my parents would have the type of relationship with my son, Aiden, I always hoped they would have. I feel bad about that for both my parents and my son.

With all that said, things have changed and improved over time. I imagine that as time continues to pass, our relationship with my parents will continue to strengthen. One might summarize family dynamics with the adage, "you don't choose your family. They are God's gift to you as you are to them." No matter what happens, I know that I'll always feel love for my parents regardless of what situations arise. I deeply respect my parents for all they did for me as a child and their dedication to raising me as an independent, confident, and determined person.

CHAPTER 11

The Pressure Builds

I quickly skimmed over the four years leading up to 2007 because I did not want to bore you with the little details of my life. We all have those little details as life happens to us, and my memory of that time is honestly like a blur. Things were moving so fast during that period in my career and personal life. Despite my personal stress (and a new baby sure adds stress!), work was just as busy as always, and the calls I responded to continued to build pressure in my professional life.

Many of my calls were collisions. Some people had injuries, some had no injuries, and some were fatalities. I was involved in many pursuits and was even engaged in a couple of service vehicle collisions where suspects driving stolen vehicles rammed my car. I investigated whatever calls came my way, from thefts to family fights to shootings and sudden deaths. I was going 1000 km/hr at work but going backwards at home. The daily stress I experienced continued to add to the weight of my baggage, but life doesn't stop because you are getting stressed out. It continues full steam ahead.

As 2007 arrived, Colette and I decided to get married in the summer. Like any good first responder, when we began to plan our wedding, I was able to direct my focus on that while I was at home. Colette loves to plan things, so she dove headfirst into the process of wedding plans. She was so meticulous that she even had a spreadsheet with the cost down to the penny! I am positive that the wedding planning was a significant distraction from any other issues we were experiencing. The wedding was sensational, and I am grateful for my wife's hard work in every detail. We had planned an outside wedding ceremony in her uncle and aunt's farmyard; they were terrific and accommodating. Colette's uncle and cousins built a beautiful gazebo we used as a stage and for pictures. We were so fortunate and grateful to everyone who pitched in to help set up, decorate, make the meal, and help with the pancake breakfast in the morning. We had a beautiful day with temperatures around forty degrees Celsius, clear skies, and *no wind* (rare for southern Saskatchewan!). It was such a great day surrounded by great friends and family, and man, did we have the party to end all parties. Our guests still talk about that wedding party that seemed to last forever, and the memories of that night are fantastic.

Life was moving along smoothly for us despite some bumps along the way. The difficulties with becoming new parents passed, and Aiden settled into being a happy little toddler. At the same time, Colette and I moved our lives forward in wedded bliss. On the surface, things seemed perfect, but they were far from it. The stress that had accumulated over time grew. Things might have boiled a bit to the surface, maybe in the form of my disengagement at home or the grumpy and closed-off way I sometimes acted. However, there were definite signs that the tinder was dry and all it took was the right-sized match to set it on fire.

CHAPTER 12

Coming Full Circle

That brings us back to the night of my shooting when I was on patrol, which happened only a couple of months after our wedding day. The event lasted maybe forty-five seconds, but it has impacted my life forever. It has changed my entire trajectory and path and is my single, most prominent memory.

After discharging my weapon at the driver, the vehicle about to crush and kill me suddenly veered away. I watched the truck drive slowly down the highway. I remember coming back to target, looking at the back window and thinking, the threat is over; it's not a movie. Get back in the car. I jumped back into the patrol car, and my partner asked me what had just happened. I said, "I shot that guy," and she replied, "you did what!?"

As my partner tried to process what transpired, I took over the radio calls for assistance. We pulled in behind the truck, but it picked up speed, so we began a chase. Despite being in a lethal threat encounter, I also took over radioing the details of the pursuit as my partner was unable to while mentally processing the unfolding situation. We were travelling at high speeds, over 160 km/hr in winter in Alberta, which is as ridiculous as it is dangerous. I was so focused in those moments, and my thoughts were singular. I was driving and making radio calls, but everything was so fluid that it felt like water as it flowed over the top of a waterfall. When I spoke to my squadmates, they all said that there was something very different with the initial radio transmission. All stopped right where they were to wait for our location. A few stopped in the middle of intersections, while some gravitated north because we were working in Sector One. We chased that vehicle until we had the assistance of Air 1 (our police helicopter), who took over the surveillance of the car from the air. The chase moved through St. Albert, where my sergeant threw a spike belt, and we were able to hit a couple of the tires. The suspects continued to loop into North Edmonton and then back into St. Albert. There were multiple units on the chase from West Division and North Division. I began to think that I must have missed the driver when I fired my service pistol because he was driving like a maniac, and the chase was going on for a long time.

The suspect hit two spike belts and ran on rims for twenty-seven minutes before finally grinding their vehicle to a halt, with only two tires remaining partially intact. At the termination point, the suspects were extracted from the vehicle one at a time except for one person lying on the truck's floor in the back seat. He was not moving. I was not at the termination point because I made a wrong turn and had to go around. By the time I arrived, all the people were in custody, and one received first aid for a gunshot wound. As I aimlessly wandered at the termination point, someone mentioned that the guy who got shot was sitting in the back seat. I was so confused because I did not shoot at the rear passenger; I shot at the driver trying to kill me! Although I seriously second-guessed my actions—in my head—I knew there was no way I could justify striking the rear passenger with a bullet intended for the driver.

Other officers arrested the truck driver, and a male found in the back seat was seriously injured and required immediate medical assistance. However, the twenty-seven-minute chase didn't favour him, and we arrested the rest of the occupants without further incident.

After the dust settled and things calmed down, my sergeant approached me. He said that just because he spoke about officer-involved shootings did not mean I had to do a live demonstration. He then took my gun and gave me his to put back in my holster. He then directed me back to the starting point of the chase and asked me to point out exactly where I was when all of this went down. That task was impossible, but I could generally point out where I was parked when this happened. He then sent me to the station to await the investigators from the RCMP in Red Deer and do what they needed to do. I have had adrenaline dumps before, but nothing could have prepared me for the size and intensity of this one. I had this massive adrenaline boost. During the event, I experienced auditory exclusion and the sense that time slowed right down into milliseconds feeling like minutes. Everything seemed acutely focused, the sharpest I have ever seen. The interaction with the truck and the shooting took forty-five seconds. Still, it felt like a few minutes, just as smooth as everything felt earlier, like the waterfall, the free fall and crash, and white-water turmoil came next.

Things began to settle after the extreme high in adrenaline, and I experienced the shakes. My hands were shaky, my body trembled, and my heart felt like it would burst out of my chest. Now that it was all over, I had this massive adrenaline dump. After that, everything came back to "normal," but really, it went the other way, just as far low as I was high. It felt like being at the bottom of that waterfall inside the white water, spinning in a circle, being pushed down, unable to break free for air. I was disoriented. I felt like crap. I was exhausted and irritable, and my body felt numb. I could have fallen asleep standing up. I waited for the RCMP for about six hours at West Division Station, and all I wanted to do was go home and get some sleep. When they finally arrived, they made a few attempts to interrogate me. I declined to answer until I spoke with a lawyer. They seized all the clothing I was wearing and then sent me home. After my initial meeting with the investigators, I was sent home for a mandatory three-day leave as per policy.

The following three days were the worst days I experienced in my entire career and my life as I remained inside that white-water wash for those days. I was treated like the bad guy and felt I had no support from the service that employed me. They told me I could not talk to anybody, and even if I could, I didn't know anyone who had experienced something like this. My wife and I received no direct support from the service. They also directed me not to speak with my partner because we needed to be interviewed by the RCMP. During those three days, I experienced a wide range of emotions, from anger to fear. I felt down, sad, and disappointed, but mostly, I felt alone and isolated. Those latter two feelings drove me into a place that seemed impossible to find my way back from. That was my iceberg. I was the Titanic, just floating in the water, playing music, thinking it's not that bad, not realizing I was ripped open down the keel under the waterline.

After those three days of administrative leave, I had my regular four days off, and I was back to work as Temporary Acting Sergeant leading a squad. There was no debriefing, counselling or programs offered to me or my family. Looking back at that time in my life, this lack of support seems shocking because we now do things differently in the police service after these types of situations. But that was the way it was back then. Shootings in the world of policing in Edmonton at that time were rare.

Additionally, things are hard to figure out when you are inside that type of situation and its fallout. It is hard to know what you need, and I had such a heavy backpack of emotional baggage that I could not even see the forest for the trees. I had no more channels left to use as they were all full.

In addition to all the internal stuff, the feeling of being let down by the service, and not knowing what I needed most, I became very angry with everything. I was angry with the people I was dealing with, the service, and the media. I became increasingly distant at home because I could not recharge and was not processing anything. I had become a storage tank. I would come home from work and zone out. I remember when I was on the couch, and the TV was on. I was sitting there, and although present in my body, I was not there consciously. Aiden, my son, tried to get my attention. He stood right beside me, tapping me on the leg, saying, "Dad, Dad, Dad, Dad, Dad." He must have said it over ten times, and Colette had to yell at me to answer and pay attention to our son. He would try hard to get my attention, standing right there in front of me. The crazy thing about that was I did not see or hear him. I was not trying to ignore him. I honestly had no idea he was even there. I was shutting down from the inside out, unable to recognize the trouble I was in at that moment.

When I remember being interviewed by the RCMP and explaining what happened to me during this event, I broke down crying. In the interview, I cried when I explained that I could have lost my family and that my son could have grown up without me. The overwhelming feeling of sadness was unbearable. Logically, you would think that because I felt like this, I would be trying my hardest to be present so I could experience all the things I was afraid to lose. But it was just the opposite. I was stuck in a loop of fear and my mind shut down. I had difficulty getting solid, restful sleep, my dreams intensified, and it was like my brain was so overwhelmed that it shut off. I ran scenario after scenario in my mind. I thought of fighting through this; if I ended this, she might be better off. It was like a never-ending game of tug of war in my mind. At my lowest point, I believed my family would be better off without me because I was becoming a burden. So, my coping mechanism was to shut off the outside world when I got home. Colette was disappointed and angry with me and my lack of action. She covered for me for a while and lived her life as a single mom. But these behaviours or solutions are only ever temporary at best. People can only ignore the elephant in the room for so long.

CHAPTER 13

Becoming Aware

I developed a few more traits because of my inability to deal with the traumas that had piled up. One of the things that I acquired was a sense of mistrust of people, and I was hypervigilant. I could not trust people, and I could not make friends outside of the policing world. I wouldn't even talk to you if you weren't wearing a uniform. I only hung out with other police officers. I was pessimistic about life, sitting in the victim mentality. I blamed my struggles on all the situations I faced. I hated the service and was very angry with everything around it or anyone who spoke highly of it. I began to hate people, the people we dealt with daily in patrol, and people in general. In retrospect, I was angry and hated almost everything. Colette was beyond frustrated, but I ignored the signs that anything was wrong. The trauma rippling under the surface had bubbled up and over and flooded my life. I was unmotivated to do things; I lost the passion I once had and didn't do anything for myself. Colette and I lived in turmoil in private for about two years after my shooting. Together we became good at masking the troubles to the outside world. I had lost my direction and lost my purpose in life.

On the surface, everything from the outside looked okay, and things were fine while I was at work. However, I experienced a physical change on the days that I was working. When I would roll up my uniforms, I felt my energy returning to my body and was more awake and aware. When I headed to work, I would feel the adrenaline start to flow, and when I walked through the doors, I would be hyperalert. I would be hypervigilant for eleven hours, four times per week. Then, when I got home, I would crash with that dump of adrenaline and be out of touch and out of my body for the four days I was off. I would go through the motions but not connect with anyone at home. I felt disappointment, sadness, and fear, but when anyone asked how I was doing, I would say, "I am good," but I was not.

The thing that assisted me from a work standpoint was that I was fortunate to be at the receiving end of good circumstances. As I mentioned, I was at the point of hating people while on patrol. However, my superiors asked me to take a detective role inside the division in a new unit. It gave me a twelve-month reprieve from the pressures of patrol work, which I needed even though I had no idea I needed it.

As I mentioned at the beginning of this, the first step was awareness. As humans, we often go through life and have experiences affecting us over time, which is a slow burn. It is just like the boiling frog theory. The theory states that if you put a frog in a pot of water that is cold and place it on a burner, the water increases in temperature slowly. The frog does not notice it and does nothing to escape, so it boils to death. The reason is that the frog does not recognize the slowly changing danger before it's too late. That was just like me; I had no awareness of all the things I had experienced as dangerous to my mental health. As a result, the damage progressed slowly and imperceivably until that night in December, when everything changed. That call for service brought me to my knees; it was my last straw. Suppose I had received some information about the importance of being aware of my feelings and what I was experiencing. In that case, I might have been able to make changes and help myself before things went off the rails.

Once I started reflecting on my career, I had to increase my awareness to include all the events that caused additional stress. I had to be honest with myself. Not exactly comfortable when I had to lay everything out on the paper in front of me. Being self-aware is something that I work on daily. I am not always successful with this, but I still try to have the daily discipline to be aware of my feelings and how I show up every day. I do my best to show up as the person in my vision, the person I see as myself.

The second thing I did was acknowledge that I had a problem, which was such a hard thing to say out loud. I took responsibility for my behaviour; I decided to take responsibility for my response to all the situations that caused me to struggle. I decided to move out of the victim mentality and live intentionally. That was not something I could do overnight, it was a slow change, and there were many baby steps. I did not understand why I was feeling the way I was, and I would not go to the doctor for anything, let alone for my mental health, so I did all of this on my own. I am not sure it was the best decision initially. Still, I have come to a good place in my life with a much deeper understanding of who I am, filling me with gratitude.

At the start of my recovery, my saving grace was my wife, Colette. I have no idea where I would be right now without her, fourteen years later. She had such tenacity and courage to take that stand for herself and the life she wanted to live. She sat me down one day, and I don't remember exactly when it was, but it was a couple of years after the shooting, and we were at the end of that road I was on. She had had enough of my bullshit. I do remember the words she spoke. She said she was done with living the way we were; she was tired of having two children to care for (one being me). Colette told me she needed help with the daily household activities that she was doing alone and needed support and a husband she could count on. She also said that if things did not change, she would be done being with me and being my wife. As we spoke during this conversation, we were full of emotion; I was ugly crying, and so was she. Even as I write this now, I feel tears well up, but now it's out of gratitude, not despair and sadness. I had to acknowledge that I almost destroyed a second marriage and the emotional impact all this had on our son.

Remember when I said there is power in a decision? There I was, faced with a decision and arguably the most crucial decision of my life. There was an immense fear inside me that I would be unable to make the required changes. I feared not knowing where to start and feared not knowing if the changes would even work to repair the damage done. It would have been easy to say I would change, shape up for a short while, and then fall back into the same old routine because it was comfortable. I was familiar with living that way. As I sat there with my head full of everything, and it was noisy inside my head, I mustered up all the remaining courage I had inside me and made the decision. I decided to face the fear head-on, making the most significant change of my life. I decided to change myself and to live better and do better. I was committed to making these changes but had no idea where I would start.

Then something almost magical happened; once I made this decision, the Universe started to conspire for me and present me with opportunities to learn and change. And once again, Colette was the catalyst for the most significant breakthrough in improving our marriage. She asked me to read the Five Love Languages book. I don't care to read, but I was committed to making real change. So, I decided to pick up the book, read it, and when I finished, I realized I was not speaking her love language. But, I have to say it was an easy read, and it gave me insight into the first few steps I needed to take to start that change.

Let me tell you a story. Before reading *The 5 Love Languages: The Secret to Love That Lasts* by Gary Chapman, I had no idea what her love language was. Before this book, I believed that when you wanted to do something nice for a spouse, you bought something for them; that was what I thought she wanted. It was Easter, and things were not great in the house, so I bought Colette, a bunch of flowers, specifically tulips, on my way home from work. I thought they were nice, and tulips signified spring and new life, and I was excited to give them to her. When I got home, I gave her the wrapped flowers, and when she opened them, she was furious. She was so upset that I gave her flowers, and then she said she hated tulips. They were the flowers she hated most. She started to cry, and I had no idea what just happened, so instead of exploring that, I got angry, and we had a little fight over the flowers. The day was destroyed before it even started.

After reading this book, I fully understood why she reacted the way she did. Her love language at the time was acts of service. All she wanted from me was to show up and help her around the house. She needed me to show her that I loved her in that way. All I had done by buying tulips was to confirm that I never listened to her when she told me she hated tulips. She just wanted me to help her and not buy something insignificant to her to show my love. While I write this memory down, I chuckle about this because now she likes tulips and likes receiving tulips or any flowers.

Reflecting on that moment, I realize our fight was not just over the tulips I purchased. It was about my inability to show Colette I loved her in a meaningful way for her. That is the thing about relationships; as any partner in a relationship knows, we each must understand that it is not always about us. It is about how we see love, not how our partner may see love. Individually, we must be able to communicate what we need from the other person. That communication is, above all else, the key to building or rebuilding any relationship. The second thing that should be a 1B is removing our ego and taking responsibility for actions rendered. Doing these two things forms a platform for real change and improvement if you are committed to making the improvements. Another important thing to remember is that our love language might change once things improve. That means we must always communicate and be aware of how things progress.

After reading this book, I also realized my next steps to make those changes. I had to be diligent in helping Colette out around the house. I decided to take my first small action steps. My goal was always to progress, not perfection, but to be consistent with those steps for my recovery and a better life and marriage. I started to help around the house by paying attention to taking out the garbage, picking up the dishes, and practicing gratitude every day. I began to open my eyes and became aware of those two seemingly, little insignificant things. I was not perfect while implementing these changes; I stumbled a lot. But I always put my best foot forward and gave 100 percent effort. The important thing about this was that I wanted to make these changes, but I had to show myself grace. I was battling an undiagnosed case of PTSI, so I focused on one thing at a time to make the required changes. I tried to be engaged at home and listen to what was needed every day. I also started my day and ended my day with gratitude by writing in a journal. By making gratitude a habit, I started my day with good energy. The power of gratitude helped me see what I had, which took my attention away from all the pain and things I did not want.

As things progressed, I would take up additional tasks, listen to what she needed, and do the requested things. I had a lot to repair and was willing to do the dirty work to smooth things out. Finally, things started to get better around the house, but I had a habit of living in the past and feeling the guilt I still carried. However, the one thing I did consistently was to remove the idea I was a victim. I replaced it with believing I was responsible for everything I did and how I behaved.

Things were going okay at work, but as anyone going through the battle to heal your mind knows, there are good and bad days. I felt much better about people and had much less anger towards the public than twelve months prior. My superiors asked me to move from the detective role into a patrol sergeant role, which they promised me for twelve months. As I said before, there were good and bad days, and there were still situations that were not working out for me.

Looking back on it now, I know my old paradigm and way of thinking was trying to bully its way back into my head. One of the situations that came up was when I applied for a promotion and was denied. I had been denied two times for promotion out of the West Division. Initially, I was angry about that, and the feeling of being a victim started to creep back in. The next thing that shook my newfound confidence was when I was bumped out of that sergeant role because a substantive sergeant wanted the position after I had it for only nine months.

There were a few more bad days, and things were not great as he moved into the role. I tried to help him integrate, but his style and my style did not mesh. Half of the crew liked him, and the other half didn't; half didn't want me to be back in that role. It was a recipe for disaster. Finally, one day it all came to a head, and he and I had this epic yelling match in the hallway outside the parade room, nose to chin because he was way taller than me. That was the end of my time in that squad. I moved into another sister squad with a new sergeant. Even though it felt good on the outside, I felt terrible. I have never apologized for this altercation, but I probably should. The sergeant with whom I had differences is a good dude, and we had different perspectives.

That was a bad day for me, and I could easily blame what happened that day on PTS. However, although it was a contributing factor, I took full responsibility for my actions. At that moment, I was quick to anger, and then I would, in the words of the CHAMP, "Lose it, snap!" Many of those moments when I lost my head were partially due to stress overload. However, I had made a lot of progress and changed how I thought, and I took responsibility for my role. I picked myself up, dusted myself off, and again started to do better.

I have learned that we can control only a few things in life, one of which is how we react to the situations we face. So I moved squads and called out my behaviour to the new sergeant. I decided to be a good follower, put my head down, and do my job. I enjoyed that squad; the people were great, I developed some great friendships, and we had fun. The sergeant and I had a great working relationship to top it off.

Looking at it from a divisional level, I had to work hard to make amends to my reputation, which I had worked so hard to achieve in the first place. I am sure to others I appeared to be a ticking time bomb, but the funny thing was no one even asked if I was okay or why I acted in a way so out of character. However, maybe that was how I always reacted, which is why no one asked me about it. To realize that is a little bit disappointing because I had a very different perspective of my behaviour in my head. The thing about having resiliency and struggling with mental health is that the way it shows up is unique for each of us. The symptoms are similar but how we show up with it is specific to the person. My particular trauma was not because of one or two bad calls; it was their cumulation through multiple years and built very slowly over time. I had no idea I was even in trouble when I was inside that feeling. It may have been evident to others looking from the outside but not to me. I had changed over time slowly, and that change was imperceivable to me. The way it is in policing, with constant change inside squads and with people you work with, no one probably noticed. So with this setback in West, I prepared for a divisional transfer to North Division.

I watched Colette make massive progress with her mindset and personal development during this time. I started to see a gap between her and me even though I was still working on myself. I was looking for other ways to better myself and close the gap between us. It was not for the competition; I saw the potential for healing and a better life. I was beginning to feel excited about the future possibilities for my family and me.

As this time progressed, I was intrigued by mindset and what that could do for me on my journey. From there, I read a book called *The Secret* by Rhonda Byrne about the law of attraction. That book opened my mind to the possibilities of changing circumstances by changing my thoughts daily. It opened the door for me to think about intentional living and doing things that help me heal by doing them intentionally. Again, I was in the zone of gobbling up information and the need to learn about myself and my mind. I then read a book by a Canadian author, Eddie LeMoine, called *Bring About What You Think About*. This book was also very good, and it expanded my mind. I took from the first time I read these books that the Universe wants all of us to succeed and what we train our minds on is what we produce in our lives.

Suppose we focus on negativity and everything that can go wrong in life. We see that we only accurately observe confirmation from the world around us that what we have focused on is true. If you want to try it, there is a quick test of this theory. When you head out of your house to run around, focus your mind on one type of vehicle, like a VW Beetle, and then in your travels, take note of how many times you see those darn punch buggies. You will likely be surprised at how many you see. So ultimately, if we think like garbage, we get garbage results. However, it is quite the opposite if we look for all the good things and what will go right in life. We are then presented with all the evidence in the form of opportunities.

The key to thinking with this mindset is recognizing those opportunities. At that moment, we can decide to step into them or not. The trick is to realize that life or the Universe will not, and I repeat, WILL NOT just give it to you. It shows up, and it's up to us to take action when it does. If we do this, then we get something fantastic in return. As you read this, you may think this is ridiculous, but look back at the last few pages of this book; there is proof there. When I started this healing journey alone, I had no idea where to start, but I was focused and intent on getting better. Then I was given the OPPORTUNITY to read *The 5 Love Languages: The Secret to Love that Lasts*. I was then given another opportunity to read *The Secret* and a third opportunity to read *Bring About What You Think About*. All these opportunities showed up, and all I had to do was make that decision and be intentional with my thoughts. I then had to take the action step to read the books and use them to move me forward.

After reading these books, I started implementing more open communication with Colette and focusing on what I wanted in life. I chose only to see the positive, use gratitude, and create better habits. I communicated that with her in a way I never thought possible. We became strong together, which I had been working towards for many years; when this happened, it took five years of small steps, hard work, and determination to get here. It was unbelievable; it was amazing to come from a place of absolute chaos and ruin to where we were. I believed in myself, in her and our family.

We even devised a plan for when I came home from my shift. The plan included giving me anywhere from ten to twenty minutes of decompression before asking me how my day was and before asking me to do something around the house. Then, if she happened to have a crappy day, she would let me know, and I would have time to decompress after I relieved her from what she was doing when I got home. One thing was certain, I always had time to unwind, and she always received the help she needed.

The things at work were still happening. I was still responding to calls for service, seeing people at the worst moments in their lives, and experiencing death and destruction every week. I also wanted a promotion and tried to get promoted to sergeant. I had gone through the promotion process three times before implementing these tools in my life and was unsuccessful. When I reflected on those processes, I focused on all the things that could go wrong and what I did not want, and ultimately, I did not get promoted. I entered the process for the fourth time and decided to focus on gratitude and all the good things in my life. I also kept things in perspective. I loved working in uniform on patrol, and I had great people around me, so even if I did not make it, I was still in an exceptional place. I kept my mind on success and visualized receiving that call telling me I got promoted. I got that call and was promoted to patrol sergeant in 2015. It was exactly what I had said I wanted; I wanted to supervise a squad, and that is where I went, in West

Division, Squad 8. I had confirmed to myself that this stuff works with the right mindset. That was the first time I saw the true power of a change in attitude and realized that resiliency was not something you could learn about and be done with. Resiliency is something that everyone needs to work on and continue to work on daily.

After I received the promotion, I was sent to West Division and became the sergeant in charge of a patrol squad. That was what I had envisioned as the perfect job for me. I impacted a group of police officers and helped them achieve their career aspirations. I was very grateful for that opportunity. I then focused on the squad and showing up for them. It was a wonderful place at work. I fulfilled the call for service in public and the members I supervised, receiving a lot of joy while performing my duties as described. My mindset change also paid off at home; we were happy and satisfied.

Things continued to improve for Colette and me. I was more connected with Colette and our son, we had better communication, and things were starting to get comfortable. When our communication improved, our relationship rose from the ashes; I felt like I had achieved what I set out to achieve. So I took a breath, sat there at that level, and admired myself for making the change I had made. I was proud and thought, yeah, man, I have arrived; I am here, and now it is time to go on cruise control.

I felt like I had closed the gap Colette had created in our early years. Still, the best thing about a healthy relationship is that there is always room to improve. That was one of the first lessons that I had to embrace after reaching what I thought was the end of my journey. Colette was always looking for ways to improve. She was happy with where we were but not completely satisfied. Somebody would soon show me another opportunity that would again change the course for us. And somebody gave us something I never knew I wanted or even dreamed about.

When I began to change things, we opened a photography business, and it was something that Colette liked to do. We invested time and money into the business, thinking that this would be the way to increase our household income. We went at it with 100 percent effort and no idea what we were doing or how to run a business, so there was a bunch that we had to learn by mistake. There were quite a few wonderful couples that we photographed for their weddings. It was fun initially, but taking photos took its toll as time passed. After a few years, Colette realized she wasn't happy being a photographer. She still loved taking pictures but not as a business.

Colette searched for where her heart was and what she believed she was meant to do. However, she never shied away from trying new things and saying yes to new opportunities. One of these opportunities showed up in the form of an MLM company.

Colette, who has had an autoimmune disease since she was fifteen, was looking for natural ways to improve her health. She was introduced to Young Living Essential Oils. She decided to get involved with the primary objective to make us healthier as a family, with an option to earn an income possibly. Not knowing where this would take her, she came to me to see if I was okay with her moving into this. I learned over time that things show up in life at different times for unknown reasons. However, I felt like this opportunity could benefit her and our family. Therefore, I supported this opportunity because it was worth the investment if it worked to help her be healthier.

During her early time with the company, she attended one of their conventions in Calgary. She went with her best friend from high school, and her friend made her change one of the sessions that they had booked to listen to two guys speak about a thing called Oola. She had never heard of this and had no idea about these two Oola Guys, Dr Dave Braun and Dr Troy Amdahl. After that session, she texted me and said we were going to Texas. Of course, I replied with a bunch of question marks. Colette said she would explain when she got home, but I could tell she was excited.

I remember vividly that she was ecstatic about Oola when she returned home. She explained how the two guys who spoke and founded Oola were terrific, and they had written a book that we needed to read, *Oola: Find Balance in an Unbalanced World*. She had this energy I had never seen before, and she mentioned how she would love to do what they do. She had mentioned that they do a conference they call Oolapalooza, and she said she would love to attend one.

We took a step that we could make at that moment, and since money was tight, we decided to order the book first. When it came in the mail, we both read it. It was such a good read; it was one of the best books for combining mindset, gratitude, and action steps that I had read. After reading the book and understanding it a little, we started implementing various steps of Oola into our lives. We did things like making note cards with something they call skittles and oranges, and we set goals in the seven areas of life based on the book. The Oola platform made sense and gave me more things to think about because it opened my mind to rounding out my life and having a balance in life that I had never had before.

If you are wondering what Oola is, I can provide a definition. First, Oola is derived from the French word Ooolala, defined as when your life is balanced and growing in seven key areas: fitness, finance, family, field, faith, friends, and fun. It is about finding balance in this unbalanced world we face daily.

I saw similarities and themes in every book I read, and I felt like I was on to something. I was very interested in this, but my curiosity and desire to explore what I saw were fighting with my cop brain, kicking in and providing me with doubt and skepticism. I think most police officers and first responders have a natural tendency to be cautious and skeptical. So when something new or different is presented that allows our minds to stretch, we fall back into what feels comfortable and what we know. I have learned over time that the only thing constant in life is change, and we can change for the better or, the worse, but that is up to you to decide which direction you want to go.

The discontent with taking photos grew, and one photography contract solidified this feeling that Colette was done. We were taking photos for my sister's dance studio in Saskatchewan a few months after she had heard the Oola Guys speak, and she got sick on the first day that we were in that town. She was so ill that she could barely get out of bed. I got the call, and I felt like I was brought up from the minor leagues, and it was my time to shine! I had to take all the photos that week. She had trained me in photography. I was always involved in taking photos as a secondary shooter at many other events, so I felt confident I could do an excellent job for the week.

So, I took the reins and shot the photos, but our sales dropped by 50 percent because she did not take the photos. We put a lot of work into those photos, which were of the same quality and level of professionalism as the previous years but without the same result. So, after that week, she took time to search deep down to figure out if photography was what she was supposed to do. She realized that she never really had that high level of passion for photos as a business. This realization caused a tremendous uneasiness because she had invested so much into the company that she felt guilty about quitting.

A little while later, she was reminded on social media that the Oola guys were hosting that event called Oolapalooza, and she knew, deep down, she had to go. She approached me, and we discussed dissolving the photography business and trying something new. She asked if I would go to Oolapalooza with her; I was game. She said the only way we would go was if she was able to sell her photography equipment to pay for the trip and the tickets. At this point in my life, I learned a couple of things: the power in deciding and opportunities show up for us to either take or let go. I also learned to trust Colette and say yes when she has these outside-of-the-box ideas.

So, we decided that if she sold all her photography equipment, we would fly to Dallas, Texas, for this event. I figured that if the conference sucked, at least I could explore Dallas and Fort Worth, so in my mind, it was a win regardless. The other thing about Colette is when she says she will do something, she usually does. So, after deciding to do this, the universe conspired with us. She sold her equipment within a couple of weeks, and we were off to Texas.

We attended the Oolapalooza, and I went into the event with an open mind. The first day was more challenging than the second, mostly because I had to get honest with myself and answer many questions about where I was in my life. I felt terrible, inspired, and excited at the same time. The entire event resonated with me; it clicked with how the Oola Guys described everything.

Overall, this event forced me to be thorough, bring the awareness piece to the forefront of my mind again, and evaluate things from where I was. Part of developing my awareness was answering questions about myself in those seven key areas of life: fitness, finance, family, field, faith, friends, and fun. I had to rate these answers out of ten, then plotted them on a wheel, and when I connected the dots, I drew nothing resembling a circle. It hit me at that moment, and I felt shame, sadness, and a feeling of despair. I felt sad for everything I had put my family through and guilty for not being able to recognize what was happening. I started to cry and release those emotions I had bottled up inside.

It was then that Dr. Troy said that the wheel only represents where I was and not who I was. Let me repeat that; it was WHERE

I was, not WHO I was. It was as if he was speaking directly to me for my growth and benefit. Additionally, at this moment, I was completely aware of where I was. With that power, I could decide to make changes to improve myself. And that is what I did. During this Oolapalooza, I learned how to set goals properly and what was stopping me from achieving those goals. I had never looked at goal-setting from the perspective of my whole life.

It is vital to set goals in all areas of our lives. Usually, most of us only set work, finances, and fitness goals. Those goals that we set traditionally come from spoken New Year's resolutions. Those goals usually fall short by March for all of us because life "gets in the way." The key was that I could see my entire life, including all the seven Fs: fitness, finance, family, field, faith, friends, and fun.

Now I know that some of you reading this will have excuses for not setting or achieving the goals you talk about, and you probably think there is no way to work on your life that way. Others will say, "I don't have time to work on myself or set goals because of ..." (You fill in the blank for whatever excuse you have.) So, I am going to call you on your crap right here. If having a better, more fulfilling life that contains more balance is something you want, then I am telling you that you can make it happen. It doesn't matter what is happening with your life if you follow this framework around living life with purpose and passion and taking action steps. An Oola life is possible for everyone.

Did you know that if you write down the goals you want, you are 80 percent more likely to achieve those goals? So, I suggest that if you take the time to write them down and put them in a place where you can see them daily, you will achieve more goals and be closer to the life you want to live. You may not write down every goal, but one or two is a start.

Some of you may feel guilt creep in because we don't usually work on ourselves; we typically work on everyone else and help everyone else. Then, we decide to skip working on ourselves. This trait is imbedded into all front-line workers, and it is a big part of our personalities. Helping others is reinforced and ingrained in us from the first training day. I can speak specifically with my training, and there have always been life priorities, and we are number three on that list. I also believe first responders tend to put others first regardless of the specific profession. Because we have that natural, built-in disposition coupled with the training received by first responders, we are terrible at asking for help. We are stubborn when facing our own situations, and we tend to deflect our problems away and focus on someone else.

I learned something during my first Oolapalooza. Dr. Troy said something that hit me, which stuck in my head. He said, "Working on you is not selfish; it is selfless because we cannot truly help anyone else until we help ourselves." It was such an interesting statement, and it got me thinking. This concept made sense as I contemplated what he said, making me feel at ease. After accepting this statement to be true, the pressure and guilt I felt fell off my shoulders, allowing me to understand that I was important and needed to work on myself.

But if you are still having trouble, think about it this way. In an airplane, during the safety briefing, they mention the sudden loss of cabin pressure. The flight attendant always directs you to don your oxygen mask before helping anyone else. If you're incapacitated, there is no way to help those around you who need help. This statement applies here to exactly what I have been discussing. Suppose we, as husbands, fathers, brothers, wives, mothers, sisters, or first responders, are on the verge of self-destruction. In that case, we cannot help anyone we encounter at work or home.

After the Oolapalooza, I felt inspired and motivated to make significant changes in my life, and my goals guided those changes. When I returned to Edmonton, life stress started to show up again, but this time, I had a solid plan for the next six months. The program gave me a foundation to rely upon, and it was what I used to guide me when things got tough. That is not to say the change happened fast; no, my changes were slow. There were many, and I mean many, screw-ups and I fell down a bunch. But I kept picking myself up, dusting myself off, and taking that one step in front of the other.

Colette and I used what we learned and continued working on our relationship and removing the specific stressors we identified in our lives. I used my plan and goals and looked at things from a whole life perspective, and suddenly, things started to change and life as I knew it became terrific. I realized that I had changed my life by taking the time to work on myself. When I compared how things were the past few years, it didn't look like much from the outside. However, I felt better on the inside, inside my brain. My mind was clearer, and I felt refreshed. I paired this with the education mindset, and I felt absolute freedom and happiness inside my soul.

Colette and I reflected on our progress and how much better we were feeling by reducing stress, working on ourselves, dreaming again, and setting goals to live more passionately and purposefully. For eight years, I did the small things around the house, read books and educated myself.

I had never spoken about what I was experiencing with anyone except my wife. I did not even share things with my mom or dad, and I had never gone to the doctor to get a diagnosis. I took the ultimatum that Colette confronted me with at the beginning of 2009 and made the changes within my life to heal. Granted, when I decided to make these changes, there was not much available to members in my position. I know now that I had an occupational stress injury, and all the additional stress I experienced at home compounded my symptoms. After I reduced my home stress by making those small changes and improving our relationship, I could process the other symptoms I was experiencing. I put the anxiety I felt every time I drove to work into perspective and was able to use it to my advantage. When I felt those nerves, I would reframe the feeling of dread to what I needed to be ready to work. I used it as a motivator and energy to do my job every day at work. The nightmares I experienced slowed down, and I had them only once or twice a month instead of every day. As a result, my sleep improved quite a bit, and as most know, good things improve drastically when you can sleep.

Colette and I take stock of our previous year every year, look at the misses/losses and revel in the wins. However, my mindset took a 180-degree turn, and I see things very differently. Everything is an opportunity to learn, grow, and be grateful for what has occurred in the previous 365 days. This gratitude extends into all aspects of the year and is imperative when looking at misses or losses. Living into gratitude has the most power in what we would frame as negative because it is easy to have gratitude in the positive. The changes in my life occurred because of daily action and preparing my mind to see opportunity in all things.

During one of our year-in-review discussions, Colette asked me, "How are you living a life you love after all those years on the job? And, after all you have seen, how are you okay?"

That question got me thinking. How can I have gone through what I went through and come out better on the other side? It is a combination of many things, including the open communication that we have always had. Colette always listened without trying to fix things or offer suggestions. One of the biggest things was that she was aware when I started to change and became hostile and distant even when I was unaware. She dared to bring it up and tossed a book at me. The one thing Colette did not do was order me or tell me or demand me to read that book. Instead, she told me how she felt and what she was not prepared to live with. Colette also told me the consequences of inaction on my part. She left the decision up to me. I had to make the choice I wanted which is an essential piece of it. If our decisions are on our own, the result is usually much better than if someone tells you what to do or what decision you should make. That is just human nature.

I decided I wanted to read the books, not because she told me to, but because I didn't want to lose my family. I didn't like where I was, I didn't like where my marriage was heading, and I knew that I needed to make changes. Unfortunately, nobody else could do it for me. So I took responsibility for myself, refused to be a victim anymore, and looked to me to make the changes and do the work. I tapped into my conscious mind. But there is a subconscious aspect to all of this as well. I think I had inadvertently developed a type of pre-trauma resiliency (PTR) by subconsciously having faith in something bigger than just me. I also had a support person who forced me to become more aware of my life, acknowledge I needed to change, and dare to make that change. By understanding my emotions, sharing those feelings, and forcing myself to communicate with those closest to me—even if the conversation was difficult or emotionally charged—I experienced healing and comfort. I could change, heal, and become better by developing a better awareness of how I worked and how things impacted others. I am also never satisfied with where I am and continue working, growing, learning, and pushing myself to be better.

Colette's acquaintance showed us another opportunity as we stretched our minds and became more curious about mindset and changing the circumstances in our lives. It was not so much that she provided me with the opportunity, but Colette, as a woman entrepreneur, was invited to participate in a mentorship program through this group of successful businesswomen. She came home and said she was excited about this opportunity but did not want to work with this one person. She was very focused on not working with her. And what do you think happened? The mentorship program paired Colette with Stacey Berger, a mindset expert.

When she came home from that event, I remember that she was upset and disappointed. She could not understand why they would pair her with Stacey. I was unsure what to say, though it might not be as bad as Colette thought, and she should give it a go. Let me tell you something; the Universe conspired to have this happen. As Stacey says, this is what it looks like when it is all working out! The mentorship program started with Colette, and I was coasting. I was good where I was. I felt content and happy. I went through my daily routines and soon noticed Colette was creating distance from me again. She started to improve, her drive increased, and she again left me behind. So I asked what she was doing that was different and what I found out was she was using a system where she laser-focused on what she would love.

That opened my awareness to having a clear and concise vision for my life. I decided to attend a Vision Workshop hosted by Stacey, which was very uncomfortable. But it was excellent, and I coupled this vision with the Oola goals and the action steps every day. I began to create daily habits that increased my resiliency and developed stronger relationships. Stacey became our coach and provided the guidance and ability to continue building a life we love.

After multiple conversations, we realized others could benefit from this as time went on. We knew we were not the only ones on the front line feeling this way. With suicide rates and mental illness on the rise, we knew we needed to do something to help other families in similar situations. So, in 2018, we decided to start Benoit Wellness Consulting. We launched the Front-Line Resiliency Project to share what we have gone through and what has worked for us with the hope that it will help others in similar situations.

This project and business venture have been my second call for service, the first being as a police officer. Unfortunately, this call for service did not show up as excitement. Instead, it showed up as fear and a genuine deep gut feeling. This feeling I was experiencing was something beyond an idea; it was a calling. So when we decided to start down this road placed in front of us, I had to rely on faith that things would work out the way they were supposed to.

I say "Faith," implying that I have been a faithful person my whole life; that is a big fat nope. I did not even know I had faith or belief in a higher power. This higher power goes by many names; one can call it God, the Creator, Mother Earth, the Universe, or whatever you want. If you are an atheist, it can be a belief in science because the world's science and how it works is still more remarkable than each of us. Therefore, faith has become a much more significant part of my life. I will never say to anyone that they need to have a belief in God or follow a religion, as that is not my place. However, I believe there needs to be something you can believe in that is bigger than you. It could be as simple as fate or the saying everything happens for a reason. I make this statement because, as human beings, it is impossible to control every aspect of our lives. Not every plan goes perfectly every time, even with extensive planning. Believing in something bigger allows us to have grace with ourselves when the best-laid plans go into the toilet. It also allows us to reframe the situation to take the most positive stuff out of a terrible situation or outcome.

Let me tell you a quick story, one of the things that I remember vividly from my humble beginnings with the police was the opportunity to participate in a sweat lodge. For those unaware of that, it is a traditional Indigenous ceremony used to give thanks, heal, and purify the mind, body, and soul. The lodge is traditionally made from willow trees and has a pit in the middle for hot stones, and inside the lodge, it is pitch black. Water and sage are placed on the rocks, creating steam and heat.

I was seated at the back of the lodge, and at the time, I did not like pitch black or heat, so I was very nervous about this experience. I was inside listening to the Elder leading the sweat, and the heat was overwhelming. He spoke Cree, so I had no idea what he was saying, but an overwhelming sense of calm flooded my senses. I had recently suffered the loss of my grandfather, an Elder in my Indigenous community in Newfoundland. During that sweat, I had a vision of my grandfather, Jake. He reached out, touched me, and gave me a look that he would always be there for me.

After that sweat, I believed that a guardian angel was looking out for me. I tell you this because I would have said that I had no faith in my earlier years and no belief in anything more significant than me. But in retrospect, I did believe it was in a guardian angel. Still, I was unaware that this constituted a type of faith. Therefore, by accident, I developed faith in something bigger and more significant than myself. To cap this story off, I spoke with my grandmother, Rose, Jake's wife. She told me a couple of years ago that she prays every night. I knew this because she is diligent in saying the rosary and prayers before bed. But I did not know that she says a prayer for me every night and every other grandchild she has. So, now I have stronger faith and believe Grandma Rose provided me with divine protection over my years of policing because I could not ask for it myself. I love her so much for it and for holding space for all her grandchildren and me. We never really know how faith will show up for us, and it doesn't need to be as grand as going to church every week and praying every day. Just be open to the possibility of faith as you heal and grow.

When I look back, if I had known what I know now—and lived my best life before my shooting—I would have done many things differently. First, I would have been able to notice sooner that I was starting to spiral downward. Second, I would have been able to have the awareness that I needed help through that moment in time. Third, I would have kept my faith instead of losing it. I also would have taken more than three shifts off after the event. I would have taken that time for my family to discuss how it made Colette feel and what she was also dealing with. Fourth, I would have been able to acknowledge how I was feeling and understand the blockers that got in my way.

Finally, I would have been able to go back to those actions, the goals I set as a focal point for healing and moving forward. But as they say, hindsight is always 20/20!

Moving forward, I believe in consciously creating connections with people to aid healing. There is something to be said about having the highest possible awareness of how you live. By making conscious decisions that align with your value system, you can be happier than you realize. That leads me to something else that I find essential: core values. Most police agencies have a motto or statement that guides the police service and its officers.

Along with that statement, every officer always embraces a list of core values through training and into their career. As I "grew" up over my policing career, I realized that I had my own set of core values that I believe. I use my core values to make decisions in my life. If that opportunity does not align with my core values, I don't follow through with that decision. I also use my core values when it comes to business decisions and picking those people I want in my life as friends. By doing this, I can have meaningful connections with like-minded people because I decide consciously with purpose. My core values include authenticity, integrity, honesty, and self-development. I write my goals down and use them as my foundation to fall back upon when times get tough. I also have a life coach that keeps me growing and expanding. I prioritize everything I must do in my life and have experienced balance. If I can do this, so can all of you! I am an average person with a busy life, but I have balance, purpose, and a passion for my future.

When I boil it down to the bare bones, it is all about mindset. Everything has two perspectives. We have to decide how to view these situations, and the old saying fits here—the glass is half empty or half full. I see everything from a glass-half-full perspective. Now I am sure you're probably saying no one is that positive, and yep, you're right. I still have moments when I am pessimistic, but the difference is I do not pitch a tent in that negative energy. I have learned that I am still human, and as a human, I love awful stuff, love to complain, and see everything that can go wrong. We do this because it is easier than looking for the positive or learning moment. The difference is that I can easily change my focus because I have opened my eyes and mind to be fully aware and honest with myself. I can tell you that it has not been easy; it has been daily work. When I first started to shift my mindset and use awareness, I would be in those moments of anger and negativity for possibly weeks. But as I got better, I stayed in that space for minutes or hours, depending on what happened. So I can recognize it easier and faster, allowing me to change the energy quicker.

I want to share an exercise with you. I want you to sit on a chair with your feet on the ground. Now think about your feet on the floor. Feel the floor supporting your feet and your feet pushing on the ground. Now, change your focus to your left elbow. What does it feel like? Next, think about your butt sitting on a chair. Feel the chair you're sitting on and the weight of your body. Do you feel your feet on the floor? Probably not because you were able to change your focus from one thing to another thing upon my suggestion. So, my question is, if you can change focus so easily upon my suggestion, why can't you change your thoughts from half empty to half full? I would suggest you can do this with practice just as easily. Here is a little trick to help you; I want you to remember the words *a piece of me*. Everything that you say after the words *I am*, you are. So, for example, if you say I am so angry or frustrated, you will feel the full effect of that negative energy around those statements.

Let me show this from a personal example. My mother recently experienced a heart attack. When I found out, I commented that I was so upset about her having this heart attack. I was focused on the worst as that is where the mind goes. I was immediately aware of this statement after I said it to myself. So I replaced it with a piece of me upset about her having a heart attack. That changed my mindset just enough to be grateful that she survived and was in the hospital receiving treatment. I was grateful for all the paramedics, nurses, and doctors who helped her and saved her life. I was still sad and scared and experienced those emotions, but my head was not spinning in a negative headspace. I managed this crisis with minimal stress and made appropriate and sound decisions. I could also share my feelings and emotions with my wife effectively.

A good practice to get into is as soon as you are aware of making that *I am* statement, is to replace it. Say a piece of me is so angry, or a part of me is frustrated or whatever adjective you want to use. That shifts that energy from totally negative to only a little negative, and the rest of you is not feeling that way; it is only a piece of you. So to test this, pretend you're angry, make the two statements, and feel the difference. It also allows you to change the focus more easily by verbalizing those words. That is where I started, and slowly things changed and improved, and I still use this today, every day, and every time I hit a wall. Because as I stated before, resiliency is not a one-and-done; you don't just learn about it once. It would be best if you worked at it daily to be effective and present in your life.

I followed up the mindset piece with gratitude. I use it every day. I intend to live fully in appreciation for everything I see and experience because everything I have done has made me who I am. I am living in gratitude. I appreciate every experience I have been through, especially the hard ones. Without those, I would not have had the opportunity to rediscover my faith, strengthen my relationships and better myself. I am most grateful for my shooting. The catalyst put me on this path to help others going through similar situations and build up others who are about to embark on civil service by protecting their communities. I want to share this idea of pre-trauma resilience with the world because everyone can be affected by traumatic events. It's not if; it's when. If we have a solid foundation built prior, we are better equipped to deal with stressful situations when they happen.

Recently, Colette set up an online survey through our company about the barriers that stand in the way of police officers and frontline workers. The most prevalent one was the stigma surrounding reporting having mental health concerns. Standing up and reporting this as an occupational stress injury can have several consequences. First, it could come with removal from their work and becoming isolated. As a police officer, it could come with the service taking away their firearm. For any police officer reading, we all know how negatively impactful this act can be.

Not only are there consequences from the agencies, but there is also the internal narrative that we tell ourselves, which includes feeling shame and guilt and the feeling that you let someone down or everyone down. The feeling of being inadequate is also something that flows freely. Now I can say that the feeling of being there for my fellow brothers and sisters in blue is powerful inside me, and the police department trained that into us. I am sure it is the same throughout the first responder world.

After my shooting, there was about a year when I questioned my abilities. I questioned my ability to be there for my squad even though I performed well at the time. The way I felt after the incurred stress made me question everything. It was like the seed of doubt had become an enormous tree of doubt. Even though I felt like that, I would never tell anyone I was having trouble, primarily due to that stigma. I did not want to be seen as weak. I understand now that admitting I needed help would not have been a sign of weakness, but that is because I am in a better place now, and it's hindsight.

One faces a slippery slope if experiencing PTSD or an occupational stress injury. There is nothing worse because a label is affixed and follows people around. Herein lies the problem, reporting these stress injuries comes with issues, even if there is a significant push to end the stigma. If someone receives a diagnosis of PTSD, there is a myth that it is unmanageable. Once you have it, you have it forever and must spend your life avoiding triggers to survive. Also, if you buy into this myth, we sometimes fall into the victim mentality and end up creating a cycle that can be hard to realize and hard to change.

I believe there is a solution to all this; anyone can overcome this injury and manage it with the right mindset, determination, and support. I did not report my struggles to anyone, and I did not seek any professional help. I probably should have gone to speak to someone; it would have helped initially. I don't regret the journey I undertook on my own. When Colette gave me the speech and I knew I had to make a decision, I had to do something other than deciding. I set my mind to believe that I was the solution. I was the only one who could change; I was the only one who could best help me. I was never a victim, and I knew I had to take it one day at a time and work every day at it. I genuinely believe this was the most critical thing I did, which is the solution. I had to be the one to advocate for myself, and I had to educate myself. I then leaned on Colette as my support. I communicated my feelings and needs, allowing her to understand where I came from. She gave me grace on the bad days. I also believe in working on resilience every day, and the program we have built uses the best tools that worked for me. If I had learned these skills early in my career, I would have been better positioned to deal with the cumulation of stress. It is something that I call Pre-Trauma Resilience. If I had been able to build PTR, I could have had more substantial, more efficient Post-Traumatic Growth.

I feel the need to touch on something here as well. At times when I am working, I get triggered by a memory or exposure to something that brings back that feeling of stress, and I blaze with adrenaline, that feeling of flight or fight. I can also tell you that I still don't like doing traffic stops on diesel trucks. My mindset has helped during all of this. Because I have structured my life around the things I want and use my goals as a guidepost, I have developed confidence in all my abilities. This confidence is greater than those feelings. I also use affirmations as my self-talk and focus on the positive. I can tell you that I am constantly talking to myself, and I use my awareness to stop the negative moments and change them into positive ones. Like I said earlier in the book, resilience is not a one-and-done; it is a daily routine and practice that must happen to continue progressing. I am also here to say anyone can get here and achieve this because I am proof that we can all achieve peace and success.

I want to highlight a story that challenged this new lifestyle and put Oola to the test. I had been living by the principles of Oola, and I was gaining momentum with my mindset. But, as I mentioned, I was still working and going to calls. That day, a call originated in a different division. A male on the train platform had stabbed an eighteen-year-old who was on his way to his university classes. The complainant was seriously injured, and the initial report was that he might not live.

The suspect then fled that scene, robbed a nearby gas station, tried to stab the clerk behind the counter, and the suspect then fled. Finally, the suspect carjacked a vehicle from another person while trying to stab that person. GPS tracked the vehicle to my division. As "luck" would have it, I located the vehicle and the suspect behind a strip of businesses in the industrial area. The suspect was out of the car, frantically looking for a way into the businesses. As I arrived, he returned to his car.

I was alone, but I did not want to put the public at any more risk, so I moved in to intercept him and pinch the car against the fence so he could not drive away. I had voiced my location and knew cars were on the way to assist. I exited my vehicle and proned him out at gunpoint based upon the threat level. I attempted to update dispatch and the members but was in a dead spot and had no radio reception. He had then jumped up and tried to kick the door into my head as I attempted to grab the car radio, hoping for better reception. I reacted in time, and it just missed.

I provided more direction to the male at this point, and he got back on the ground. I then went hands-on to place him in handcuffs. As soon as I had one cuff on, the man began to fight, and it was a fight that I had not anticipated. We fought and rolled on the ground, and he ripped all the items off my duty belt; it looked like a yard sale. He and I rolled around, and he twisted around me and grabbed my sidearm in my holster, trying to rip it out. He pulled so hard it lifted me off the ground. I fought him with one hand and retained my weapon with the other. Some drug energized the suspect, and I started to fatigue, realizing I was in trouble.

I could break his grip on my pistol and gain a little distance. I deployed my OC spray, and he tried to get back into his car. I thought he might be going for his knife, so I ripped him back out of the car, and we rolled around a few seconds more, and then he was up and running. I was exhausted. I gave chase, but he was pulling away, and then I saw my back up, and they continued the pursuit and arrested the suspect.

As I gathered myself and went back and picked up all the stuff he had ripped off my belt lying on the ground, I felt the emotions I felt back in 2007 after my shooting. I was shaky with adrenaline, and I felt the self-doubt creeping in; it was déjà vu. I had been here before, and there was such a flood of emotions.

The difference was at this moment, my mind went straight to gratitude. I was grateful for keeping my cool, retaining my weapon, protecting the public from further harm, and for my backup. I brought myself back to a normal feeling with a small adrenaline dump. I was able to debrief with my staff sergeant and called Colette to communicate what I went through and what I was feeling.

The exciting thing is the feeling of gratitude continued to build for me. I experienced the feeling, and it was so positive that all the negative emotions that initially crept in stayed away. I did not have any negative feelings because of this event. The event could have been horrible for me, especially if the suspect had gotten my gun; that could have been it. He could have killed me with my weapon. That is not a great statement to hear as a cop. But, even with this reality, I was still living inside of gratitude and feeling the wonderful feeling of gratitude.

This event was a big test of Oola, the mindset work, resiliency building, and everything I worked towards. I never even lost a step towards working on my goals. I felt terrific, and I was in a good place. All I can say is that it works, so it reinforced how important it was to remain on course and showed the importance of working on resiliency daily.

I have talked a lot about my perspective in this book, and to be honest, there is a whole other half to this story. That half involves Colette and the vicarious trauma she experienced due to what I went through. I can only imagine what she felt when I told her I shot someone and then went to sleep that morning in December 2007. I feel like she is the jelly to my peanut butter in the sandwich of life. But that is her story to tell, so I will try to convince her to write it down one day.

I am now coming to the end of my career as a police officer, and I have a vision for my future that allows me to continue to serve others. Moving forward, my service focuses on all the people working on the front line. I want to give back to those still serving their communities and making them safe. I want to see their families stay together and become stronger in the process. I want them to realize the infinite potential they possess inside them and to tap into that potential.

That is why my wife and I started our company Benoit Wellness Consulting and launched the Front-Line Resiliency Project. This project aims at providing education and support to frontline workers and their families. The project's design is to go beyond awareness and shine a light on things like PTSD and suicide amongst first responders. Its design provides action and actionable steps for individuals to change their lives while consciously connecting to the larger first responder family. I learned about this stuff the hard way, but it doesn't have to be that way for you or your loved ones. If I can make this change and become more resilient and better, so can you! As I said at the beginning of the book, I am a regular guy with a story just like you. By sharing my experiences, our program and the things I use daily to improve, I hope you can take that first step on your journey of self-discovery and recovery. Or maybe you take these steps and make your family unit stronger than ever. I wish you the best on your journey, and please reach out to Colette or me if you have any questions or would like us to assist you with your goals for your future.

One thing has happened because of all this work on myself. This result shocked me because it was unintended, and the result was superb. I began this journey to heal myself, increase my family's connection, and make my family better. When I started this journey, Aiden was about three years old. I did everything to be more present and have a great home life. As the time went on and with all the work, Aiden grew up learning by osmosis and picking up tricks and tips, but I did not specifically teach him anything. What happened with Aiden was he realized that he could dream and he could follow his heart. He decided that he loved movies and wanted to be a director and producer of films. So he started to do his research about screenwriting and directing. He hated language arts in school and is now in high school. He loves that class, and he has done some fantastic things. I want to share a poem he wrote for his class for Remembrance Day. I believe it shows that anything can happen when we work on ourselves and create an environment where we can influence those around us in unique and positive ways. Here is his poem:

AFTER HE RETURNS HOME

by Aiden Benoit

Bang! Bang! Boom! Bang!
Images swirl in his head like a merry-go-round.
His hands over his eyes,
Screaming in agony
As he remembers
As he remembers it all.

The bodies, men, women, children;
The blood, pools among pools
Cover and surround the bodies,
The limbs that lay dead
Across from the body they once belonged.
Bother him then it did not, but now
He can't sleep; he dreams,
He dreams of the screams, the extensive screams
Of the victims he passed as he, with his brothers,
Walked slowly through the town in shock and disgust
about what gushed into his eyes.

His family pushed away,
The world shut out,
Alcohol the only remedy for sleep;
Drinking to keep the demons away
But deaf to the new demon
About to make him fray.

His girlfriend arrives to check-in;
Finds his apartment silent, too silent.
She enters but soon regrets,
Her face blank as she enters;
The silence is broken by a sobbing scream
A note on the table, anything but a fable.

Silence, total silence;
No more images swirling like a merry-go-round.
No more agony, just peace;
Nothing left to remember,
Nothing at all.

I could not be prouder of him. I am so very grateful for his deep understanding of the world of mental health and the consequences of not maintaining his well-being.

What I have learned from this journey over the last twelve years is there is nothing that we as individuals cannot overcome. We can achieve anything if we decide and create a clear plan with reasonable action steps. Our minds are mighty, and if you get curious about harnessing this power, there is nothing but success in your future. There is power in deciding, and when you choose from your vision, the Universe will conspire to provide you opportunities to fulfill this vision. I have also learned that having someone to keep you accountable and point out your blind spots is also critical to success. I have had a coach for business and mindset for the past four years, and this is the best investment I have ever made. The greatest gift we can give our kids is a better version of us! By giving them the best we have, by working on ourselves, we show them how to live a life they love, keep dreaming, create good habits, and be great people. They are the world's future, and we need to nurture them so they can do better than us.

A call for service almost broke me and crippled me. But the call for service saved me, drove me forward, and motivated me to give back to others.

I want to thank you for staying with me through my story. I hope that by reading this, you will have had time to reflect on your situation or have found a connection with your own story that has assisted you in some way. Know that you are not alone wherever you are in your journey, and know that you can be the champion of your story. You all have that ability to change, be resilient, do better, and heal.

I will leave you with the following analogy as a final thought.

I want you to look at the game of baseball. For those that are not familiar with the game, it is simple. A batter stands at a base, trying to hit the ball thrown at him by the pitcher, throwing the ball past the batter to strike. If the batter swings and misses the ball three times or the pitcher throws the ball past the batter over the plate three times, the batter is out. On the other hand, if the batter hits the ball, he runs to the next base and the next base until he crosses home plate to count a run. Sometimes, the batter hits the ball out of the ballpark, which is a home run. The batter can then advance around the bases to count a run. That is simple, but the game at the primary level applies to this analogy.

In baseball, the players looked up to the most can hit the ball effectively, get on base efficiently, and hit home runs more frequently. Baseball is a game of numbers and stats. The best hitters (sluggers) have a batting average of .300 or better. That means they hit the ball and get on base three out of every ten times they bat, or thirty out of one hundred, or 300 out of 1000. A ballplayer with this average is one of the best in the league, destined to be a hall of fame inductee because of this remarkable performance.

On the flip side, this means that this hall of fame hitter misses seven out of ten times. As a percentage, all this equals 30 percent success and 70 percent failure. These few players are the best in the game. The rest are below this average percentage, although they are still looked up to by many.

Suppose we were to take this and apply it to life. In that case, let's celebrate the 1 percent of the times that we succeed in life and take the opportunity to learn and grow from the misses. As we move through the game of life, we stand at the plate, and life throws opportunities at us. We have the choice to take a swing at that opportunity or to let it pass by.

We often get upset and feel like quitting the game if we swing and miss. But, sometimes, we sit on the sideline because it is way easier to do that and take no chances and watch life pass by.

Sometimes we get hurt and must sit and watch until we heal and have the chance to get back into the game. Sometimes, we stand in the batter's box and swing at the opportunity that comes our way. But, unfortunately, sometimes we only make it part of the way and fall, or circumstances change, and things don't go as planned. So the key here is to keep getting up. We must dust ourselves off and stand in the box for the next opportunity because what if that next opportunity is the one you hit out of the park, and it is a home run?

What if you didn't play the game and take that swing at that opportunity? There would be no way you could hit that home run.

But what if you did?!

Suppose you succeeded 1 percent or 30 percent of the time—you are still a Hall of Famer. I believe that we, as a society, should celebrate all the times we succeed because this is resiliency. The human spirit is to get back up and keep going after being knocked down and seize the opportunities presented from a place of love, gratitude, passion, humility, and wisdom.

My challenge to you is to answer these questions:
What will you decide today will be the catalyst for change in your life?
Will you decide on a vision?
Will you decide on better mental health?
Will you decide for your family?
Will you decide on your overall health?
Will you decide on a hobby?
Will you decide on financial freedom?
What will you decide?

With love,
Gary Benoit

About The Author

Gary is originally from Newfoundland and spent his early childhood in Alberta before moving to Saskatchewan, where he lived until 1998. At that time, he returned to Alberta soil and served the community for twenty-two years as a police officer. He is a licensed agent in the financial services industry and a Peer Support Facilitator for OSI-CAN Edmonton. Gary is also an international best-selling co-author of the book *bLU Talks, Business, Life and the Universe.* As a police officer, he saw many trying things. He was involved in challenging situations, including navigating the ups and downs of an officer-involved shooting. This incident was the breaking point of years of cumulative stress and trauma.

Gary is down-to-earth, genuine, and a dedicated and caring leader. Gary and his wife Colette own Benoit Wellness Consulting and founded the Front-Line Resiliency Project. They realize the importance of having a solid foundation, a resilient mind, a positive support system, and a balance that reduces daily stress. So now, they are on a mission to make a difference in the lives of others.

FOLLOW GARY

www.benoitwellnessconsulting.com
https://www.facebook.com/Benoitwellnessconsulting
IG: @benoitwellnessconsulting
IG: @frontlineresiliencyproject

Manufactured by Amazon.ca
Bolton, ON